Data Governance Change Management

From Drift to Direction— Why Every Data Leader Needs an ANCHOR

Aakriti Agrawal and Dr. Arvind Agrawal

Technics Publications
SEDONA, ARIZONA

TECHNICS PUBLICATIONS

115 Linda Vista, Sedona, AZ 86336 USA
https://www.TechnicsPub.com

Edited by Steve Hoberman
Cover design by Lorena Molinari
Illustrations by Joseph Shepherd

First Printing 2025

Copyright © 2025 by Aakriti Agrawal and Dr. Arvind Agrawal

ISBN, print ed.   9798898160098
ISBN, Kindle ed.   9798898160104
ISBN, PDF ed.   9798898160111

Library of Congress Control Number: 2025945395

To those who work to change the world for the better.

Acknowledgments

A huge thank you to everyone who made this book possible!

To Arvind, as my coauthor for his support and contributions to this work, and as my dad, who taught me how to change the world around me, whether in my professional career or otherwise.

To my mother, Sushma, for supporting this project and the late nights and early mornings of brainstorming, and for never letting me believe that limits existed for me!

To my mentor and friend, Danette McGilvray, for encouraging me to reach higher than I thought possible and for paving the way for women in this field and many others. Your support has been one of my greatest strengths, and I will forever be grateful for all the energy you've gifted me.

To the mother of Data Governance, and my mentor and friend, Gwen Thomas, for formalizing language in our field and charting the path for so many people in this field. Thank you for all of the work you've done and welcoming for all, and thank you for ensuring I have always felt included.

To Valerie Bonventre Calvo, John Hyun Ki Lee, Tiankai Feng, David Smith, Maria Alejandra Restrepo, and Diana Barrett, thank you for allowing us to tap into your expertise and interview you about your thoughts on change management.

To Steve Hoberman and Jenn Nichols for their hard work editing, coordinating, and bringing this to print.

To our data governance and change management friends and mentors: Tony Shaw, Deron Hook, Briana Bauer, Marilu Lopez, Laura Madsen, Len Silverston, Andrew Andrews, Mathias Vercauteren, and many others who show us how to influence and impact data governance on a daily basis.

To Joshua Kim for our new author headshots, and for all of your support.

To Nicci Peterson and Justin Stark, who taught me that community change was possible and trusted me to lead Girls Code Lincoln from the start, and to all the volunteers and partners who keep our vision alive! Thank you for allowing me to be a part of one of the most impactful changes in my career and life!

To everyone else who supported us through this endeavor, all of the friends who offered to proofread, provide input, share thoughts, put up with the crazy schedules, and just overall supported either one of us, thank you!

Disclaimer: This book is an amalgamation of thoughts by the authors and quoted interviewees, not the companies or organizations that they represent.

Contents

Note From The Authors

Aakriti

Hello! If you're holding this book, you, like me, care about leading change (or you've just entered a role where you suddenly have to lead change and are looking for help). Managing change is hard, but the need to manage change is constant, especially for data professionals. This puts us in an interesting predicament—as data governance professionals, we need to learn how to manage change effectively and efficiently.

There's no better poster child for change than me! I've been managing change my entire life. As a child, my family was always on the move, and I had to learn to adapt quickly to changing social circles, environments, and new experiences. As an adult, I founded my first nonprofit, Girls Code Lincoln,[1] at 21 with two of my friends. I experienced a need to manage change in a new way — by teaching girls computer programming, we changed how they thought about themselves and the world around them. I had to learn new skills to be successful in the nonprofit space, including recruiting volunteers and creating excitement for our

---

[1] Girls Code Lincoln is a 501(c)3 nonprofit organization that aims to close the gender gap in STEM through technology education, in Lincoln, Nebraska, USA. More at https://girlscodelincoln.org/.

mission within our community, so that people could become involved in our story.

In my first data governance role, I realized that many of my community-building skills were well-suited to the data governance space. We, too, were trying to generate buy-in internally in our corporate communities, attempting to find people who could serve as champions and partner with us to change the status quo.

Bringing these ideas together, I have been able to apply an unexpectedly large amount of my change-making experience in the corporate data space. I recognize that effective change leadership is crucial to the success of data governance programs. Along with Arvind, we have compiled all our techniques and secrets of our success into this book. We hope that this information can be used and leveraged to create more effective change within your data organizations, as well as within your communities and personal lives.

Sincerely,

Aakriti Agrawal

PS: Handouts, list of resources, and other material in relation to this book can be found on AnchorYourChange.com

Arvind

Change is the only constant that I have experienced in my long professional career. If you work on projects, as I did with product launches, you must invent, design, and change current processes to accommodate the new product. You must sell your ideas to gain buy-in among the company's decision-makers and be prepared to adjust your plans at a moment's notice based on their feedback. That means you must always be ready with a few options. Change management is an integral part of many jobs today. I was fortunate to have dealt with senior managers in the companies I worked with, as they could decide whether something I suggested was workable. So, the decision-making cycle times were short. However, today, change initiatives have fallen on the shoulders of middle managers who do not have a hand in making policy and must follow processes that may not align with their initiatives. Often, these middle managers are positioned a couple of levels below the decision-makers, so they must rely on their ingenuity to push through their ideas.

The ANCHOR model of change management is a fascinating tool for middle managers seeking to deliver excellent results while following the rules, regulations, and processes they had no hand in designing. The ANCHOR model serves as a reminder of how middle managers can assess the value of their contributions, keep themselves and their teams motivated, and continue to bring together a diverse group of people with different skill sets to deliver their jobs effectively. We have tried to share common principles through the ANCHOR change leadership model, which we found to be effective in our change-making journeys. Practitioners can apply the tools in this book in their daily lives, too. I hope you make the ANCHOR model a part of your toolkit that you can pull out at any juncture in your professional career. Please do share your successes using the ANCHOR model with us. Please also share if you have ideas to improve it or suggestions about situations where it is not effective. Your thoughts are always welcome and will help grow this body of knowledge.

Sincerely,

Arvind Agrawal, PhD.

PS: Handouts, list of resources, and other material in relation to this book can be found on AnchorYourChange.com

Foreword

I love the Agrawals! Unusual way to start a foreword, you say? Read on for the history behind my statement and why it matters to you and the subject of this book, change management.

I was introduced to Aakriti Agrawal December 2022 in Washington DC by a mutual friend and business colleague, Deron Hook. Her first words were "My name is Aakriti and it rhymes with Socrates." A helpful hint that kept me from tripping over the pronunciation. Notice her change management skills showing up in that first conversation – tying in something new with something familiar? She attended my 2-day Ten Steps to Quality Data course at the same conference, DATAVERSITY's DGIQ East (Data Governance Information Quality). Six months later our paths crossed again in San Diego at the June 2023 DGIQ conference.

Aakriti's energy and enthusiasm were infectious. She impressed me from the start. I asked her to collaborate with me to build a workshop around entrepreneurial skills for data managers, which included change management. Aakriti accepted. Our professional collaboration and personal friendship began.

I quickly learned Aakriti was just the right person to work with. She had a master's degree from University of Nebraska-Lincoln with a focus on Entrepreneurship, Leadership and Nonprofit Management. She started and grew Girls Code Lincoln, a nonprofit organization that aims to close the gender gap in STEM for girls by teaching them how to computer program. In addition, she continues to serve in advisory roles for a public university and international non-profits. She was nominated to the Forbes Thirty Under Thirty list for social impact in 2022 for her nonprofit work. Wow! All her accomplishments were unknown to me when I extended my original invitation. We went on to present a keynote, moderate a keynote panel, and teach a half-day workshop at subsequent conferences.

Our personal and professional relationship continues to this day. Aakriti's talents and knowledge still impress me. Her unique set of experiences (gained from her education, practical business experience in a large multi-national organization, her non-profit and advisory board work, and her leadership within the larger data management community) positions her well to write a book on change management.

At the same June 2023 DGIQ conference just mentioned, I had the privilege of meeting Aakriti's parents, her father Dr. Arvind Agrawal and her mother Sushma Agrawal. They came to San Diego to enjoy the weather and a short vacation. Both were delightful people who felt like long-time friends from the first conversation. Aakriti and her parents – three for the price of one! How lucky for me.

Over time, I learned that Arvind had his own qualifications in change management. He brought an international perspective from within the financial services industry. His deep skills were honed from 30 years as a marketing professional where he successfully launched many financial products. In his work he focused on the full customer experience – from pre-launch to launch to post-launch. Change management was at the heart of these large-scale initiatives. Arvind is now a full-time assistant professor at the University of Nebraska at Omaha. I greatly appreciate his friendship, intelligence, good humor, and his open and approachable manner.

Together Aakriti and Arvind developed a model for change management called ANCHOR, their six-stage framework to help lead people-centered change. I encouraged Aakriti to write a book so others could learn from their ideas and introduced her to Steve Hoberman, owner of Technic Publications. With this book you get the benefit of the Agrawals' decades of combined experience leading change. They also draw upon the experience of real data professionals and middle managers and share their insights with you. Equally important, the Agrawals stand out because of their enthusiasm and willingness to share their knowledge and true desire to help others succeed.

Why should you care about the particulars of Aakriti and Arvind? Authors of books such as this should have well-grounded ideas tested through practical experience. The Agrawals have both. Plus, they are good human beings. Change management is all about working with people. Change management will help your bottom line and the success of your data governance. But if you do not appreciate the humanity of the people behind your efforts you will be much less successful than you could be.

Why do we need another change management book? This change management book is meant for *data governance and all data professionals.* In addition, the Agrawals have identified a critical audience that is often overlooked – that of *middle management.* Those in middle management play a critical role in the success of data initiatives. They have the difficult responsibility of working between executives/senior management (who provide support, funding, and strategic direction) and their own teams (who execute plans) to ensure all pieces are aligned, implemented, and sustained. Change management needed!

If you are *new* to change management, this book is a good place to start. If you have *experience* with change management, use it to supplement what you already know. Even with the helpful focus on data governance and middle managers, this book can help *anyone* who cares about or is involved in *any* work that triggers change.

Now more than ever we need smart, kind, knowledgeable people to help us find answers to our challenges when implementing the many efforts that introduce change. To be truly successful, paying attention to the human element of our work must be at the center of any solution. Successful change management requires good methods, people skills, someone who truly wants to help, and most importantly a heart. Arvind and Aakriti have them all.

Are you convinced? Great! Read this book and (most importantly) apply what you learn for the good of our organizations, our families, our communities, our societies, our world - anywhere people are facing change. We all have a lot to do. Let's get started!

Danette McGilvray

President, Granite Falls Consulting, Inc. Consultant, Trainer, Speaker, Coach. Author of *Executing Data Quality Projects: Ten Steps to Quality Data and Trusted Information*™, *2nd Ed.* (2021, Elsevier/Academic Press). Available in Chinese and Japanese, with the Spanish translation soon to be released.

Charting New Territory

"When talking about our data governance program, we're very much using terms like 'foundational', 'incremental', and then 'transformational' to acknowledge that this change happens over time. It is evolutionary, not revolutionary, and it's meant to be gradual."

Valerie Bonventre Calvo,
Vice President of Data Governance & Enablement (Financial Services)

Importance of Change Management

In the digital world, data is increasingly recognized as one of the most important assets an organization can own. According to Statista,[2] the volume of data worldwide has grown from 2 zettabytes[3] in 2010 to 123 zettabytes in 2023. This reflects a growth rate of around 37% annually. Therefore, effective data management—ensuring it delivers maximum business value—has

---

[2] Statista - article: "Volume of data created, captured, copied, and consumed worldwide," as of May 2024.

[3] A zettabyte is equivalent to one trillion gigabytes, or a billion terabytes.

become increasingly critical. To harness the value of growing data volumes, organizations must develop new competencies such as data-driven decision-making, predictive analytics (e.g., anticipating customer needs in e-commerce), streamlined processes (to boost operational efficiency), real-time risk management, and identification of new areas for revenue generation. This shift from intuition-based decision-making to automated, data-driven decision-making necessitates changes in organizational structure and roles, the creation of new departments, and the development of new skill sets. As a result, companies are modernizing their technology systems, migrating data to the cloud, hiring and promoting employees, and dealing with rapidly evolving regulatory challenges that require thoughtful access to and management of data.

One of the fundamental needs when modernizing data and technology is the growth of data governance and data management programs. This requires data managers to lead organizational change with an entrepreneurial mindset - navigating new business dimensions often outside their traditional scope: managing upwards, downwards, and laterally; creating new programs with very little organizational buy-in or budget; and creating true changes in organizational habits in the way that data is collected, stored, processed, and utilized.

As a result of the rapid shifts in the role of data, change management has become an ongoing activity essential for keeping pace with data-centric business models. Historically, change was unpredictable. So managing change tended to be reactive, discontinuous, and ad hoc. We may not always know what is coming next. However, we need to be prepared to manage change effectively when the need arises.

We will explore the effective and proactive management and leadership of change. Change management is a systematic process of dealing with change. It involves not just implementing change, but also institutionalizing it by fostering understanding, commitment, and adoption. While most examples are rooted in data governance, these concepts are widely applicable. We have applied them in data governance, marketing, and nonprofit entrepreneurship, across fields and industries.

Data Governance Managers Must Know Change Leadership

Historically, organizations have prepared for change as a top-down and one-time initiative. According to Statista,[4] only 18% of organizations worldwide are currently highly effective in enabling change, with 64% indicating that their change management efforts are only moderately effective. Another 18% of organizations indicated that their change management efforts have failed. Organizations that succeeded in their change efforts attribute their success to a centralized project management office.[5]

---

[4] Statista - article: "Share of organizations with effective change management worldwide," as of January 2014.

[5] Statista - article: "Leading factors in sustaining organizational change worldwide", as of January 2014, by company performance.

However, a centralized project management office may not be well-suited to respond to the need for ongoing adaptation in a rapidly evolving environment. To meet this need, change management should be embraced by mid-level managers, such as data governance leaders. They manage change as a continuous process, rather than as a one-time event. It must be institutionalized as a core capability—one embedded into everyday decision-making and leadership at the middle tier of organizations.

Research[6] shows that 70% of change initiatives fail to achieve their goals. This failure is due to a variety of reasons, but often stems from a lack of appropriate leadership support and a limited understanding of the challenges that hinder success. Change requires perseverance—an ongoing and strategic effort. Change management facilitates smooth transitions to new systems, minimizes resistance to incorporating contemporary methodologies and practices, and maximizes the benefits of adopting new data management technologies. Change management also supports robust data governance frameworks by ensuring data quality, security, compliance, and privacy through the establishment of standardized data management practices across the organization.

Mid-level managers are challenged not only to motivate their teams but also to excite their peers to do what is best for the organization. They need to ensure that their project is prioritized

---

[6] https://www.mckinsey.com/featured-insights/leadership/changing-change-management.

for data governance, and then generate support from their peers for this project. They also need to advocate for these projects upwards to senior managers who provide resources for the project. They must also secure executive approval for the changes they propose. This multidirectional engagement is what we refer to as change leadership for mid-level managers. A small group of data governance experts needs to sell their ideas to business leaders, functional leaders, and senior leaders. This is change leadership in action.

While our focus in this book is on managing change within data governance, the model we share applies across many organizational functions. For example, IT needs to implement new software, upgrade existing software, modify software protocols, such as transitioning from decentralized to centralized systems, and update hardware. Changes in the business environment may necessitate upgrading business processes, such as shifting to online purchasing, remote working, online learning, and updating data security measures due to the threat of cyber-attacks. Legal changes encompass compliance with existing and new laws, as well as meeting the federal government's reporting and auditing requirements. Every department now operates in an unprecedented environment that demands changes to its processes, systems, and protocols. COVID-19 was a monumental event that turned our world upside down, forcing every organization to adopt a digital business model, serve consumers online, implement flexible work policies, and build resilient supply chains.

Take a Moment (#1)

Think about a recent instance of change, disruption, or challenge for your organization. List what happened during the disruption and your feelings about how it was handled.

What is Data?

The Cambridge[7] Dictionary defines data as facts or numbers, which are collected to be examined and considered for decision-making. Raw data, in itself, may not convey any meaning. Data may be used for reference or further analysis. Information, on the other hand, is processed, organized, or structured data. Data can come in many forms, not just numbers or words, and therefore could include symbols or characters. For example, our senses provide us with data in the form of what we see, hear, taste, feel, and more. This data, based on the context, turns into information that helps us process the world around us – what we see as we cross a busy street, feed the dog, or even drink another sip of milk that may have gone bad.

---

[7] https://dictionary.cambridge.org/us/dictionary/english/data.

In the business world, we're surrounded by data in various forms, including emails, social media, structured datasets, and even information we receive from those around us, such as near the water cooler or through informal conversations.

However, data doesn't help us make decisions without context. Context provides us with understanding, which is crucial to effective decision-making. We can't make decisions with data without intuition and context,[8] especially when the data is raw or not processed. This is where data governance comes in.

What is Data Governance?

"With these digitization projects that we have, it's easy to say a system is going to take care of problems in the future. We're going to a new system; it's going to take care of everything. Well, if you're a bad driver, it doesn't matter what kind of car you're driving. Right? So, I've had to make sure that we don't have bad drivers when we get these new cars. This involves investing in people, rather than just technology."

David Smith, Data Governance Director (Footwear/Apparel)

Data governance refers to the strategic framework and practices that manage, use, and secure an organization's data assets. Data governance involves overseeing the quality of data, assigning data ownership and accountability, ensuring data security and privacy, establishing standardized access rules and policies, and managing data throughout its lifecycle.

---

[8] https://www.harvardbusiness.org/data-and-intuition-good-decisions-need-both.

This lifecycle includes ongoing updates based on evolving business contexts and regulatory requirements, active data stewardship, metadata management, compliance monitoring, and the continued refinement of a cohesive governance framework.

Let's Talk Lingo

Throughout this book, you'll see some other data governance terms referenced, so we wanted to make sure we're on the same page with some of these:[9]

Data Stewardship refers to the formal, specifically assigned, and entrusted accountability for business (non-technical)

---

[9] These definitions are a combined creation from the DAMA Data Management Book of Knowledge, the DAMA Definitions document, as well as our personal experiences. Other references used are specifically noted.

responsibilities, ensuring effective control and use of data and information resources.

A **Data Steward** is a business leader and/or subject matter expert designated as accountable for:

- The identification of operational and business intelligence data requirements within an assigned subject area
- The quality of data names, business definitions, data integrity rules, and domain values within an assigned subject area
- Compliance with regulatory requirements and conformance to internal data policies and data standards
- Application of appropriate security controls
- Analyzing and improving data quality
- Identifying and resolving data-related issues.

Note: In some organizations, data stewards are found within the organization and given formal responsibilities while they are already working with data. In other organizations, data stewards are hired to work with data. In the latter structure, it's important to remember that a data steward may not become quickly (or ever) an expert on the data. In these instances, Aakriti likes to refer to a data steward like a librarian – they are aware of all of the books in the library and where they can be found, they know the category of the book and maybe a little bit about the story in the form of the blurb, but they haven't read them all. They understand the metadata of each book, but couldn't tell you what's on page 70.

Similarly, data stewards may know where data sits within the organization, and may even know how to find information about the data, such as the data owners or business process owners. They understand the metadata of the data, or know how to find information when needed, but they may not, themselves, be true experts of the data, as a data owner or data user may be.

A **Data Owner** is an individual responsible for definitions, policy, and practice decisions about data within their area of responsibility. For business data, the individual may be called a business owner of the data.

A **Data Custodian** is a technical data steward, responsible for handling the storage and security of a data set.

Data Lineage is a description of the pathway from the data source to its current location and the alterations made to the data along that pathway.

Data Quality refers to the degree to which data is accurate, complete, timely, and consistent with all of the requirements and business rules relevant for a given use.

Metadata refers to the "data about data", or data that defines and describes the characteristics of other data, used to improve both business and technical understanding of data and data-related processes.

Master Data is the data that provides the context for business activity data in the form of common and abstract concepts that relate to the activity. It includes the details (definitions and identifiers) of internal and external objects involved in business transactions, such as customers, products, employees, vendors, and controlled domains (code values).

Reference Data refers to any data used to organize or categorize other data, or for relating data to information both within and beyond the boundaries of the enterprise. This usually consists of codes and descriptions or definitions.

The **Data Catalog** is a repository of data assets with information about that data, giving people tools to find trusted data, understand it, and use it appropriately.[10]

Data Policy refers to short statements of management intent and fundamental rules governing data in the various stages of the Data Lifecycle.

Data Profiling is an approach to data quality analysis where statistics are used to show patterns of usage and contents.

A **Data Standard** is an agreed-upon approach to allow for consistent measurement, qualification, or exchange of an object, process, or unit of information. They are often created in conjunction with the Data Policy.[11]

---

[10] As defined by Alation, https://www.alation.com/blog/what-is-a-data-catalog/.

[11] As defined by the National Library of Medicine, https://www.nnlm.gov/guides/data-glossary/data-standards.

Data Sharing refers to the exchange of data and/or metadata in a situation involving the use of open, freely available data formats, where process patterns are known and standard, and where they are not limited by privacy and confidentiality regulations.

Data Privacy is the limitation of data access to only those authorized to view the data.

Data Security refers to the measures taken to prevent unauthorized access, use, modification, and destruction of data.

Data Classification is broadly defined as the process of organizing data by relevant categories so that it may be used and protected more efficiently. This makes data easier to locate and retrieve, and often involves tagging data.[12]

Data Architecture refers to the physical technology infrastructure supporting data management, including data servers, data replication tools, and middleware; or to the method of design and construction of an integrated data resource that is business driven, based on real-world subjects as perceived by the organization, and implemented into appropriate operating environments, consisting of components that provide a consistent foundation across organizational boundaries to provide easily identifiable, readily available, high-quality data to support the current and future business information demand.

---

[12] As defined by Digital Guardian, https://www.digitalguardian.com/blog/what-data-classification-data-classification-definition.

The **Data Lifecycle** is a conceptualization of how data is created and used, which attempts to define a "birth to death" value chain for data, including creation/acquisition, storage and maintenance, use, movement to archive, and destruction/deletion.

A **Data Governance Council** refers to the highest-tier data governance organization in an enterprise. It includes senior managers serving as executive data stewards, along with the data management leader and the CIO. A business executive may formally chair the council as chief data steward, with the data management leader serving as the facilitator for council meetings and other activities.

The **Data Governance Office** is a staff organization of full-time data analysts found in larger enterprises whose mission is to support the Data Governance Council and the Data Stewardship teams and their efforts.

Data Ethics encompasses the moral obligations of gathering, protecting, and using personally identifiable information and how it affects individuals. Some of the pillars of data ethics include ensuring that an individual has ownership over their own personal information, ensuring transparency on your company's methods or intentions with relation to data, keeping data private and in accordance to all relevant laws and regulations, ensuring data is collected based on good intention and for a good purpose, and ensuring that outcomes of data are in alignment with avoidance of harm.[13]

A **business glossary** is a collection of data-related terms described in a clear language that everyone in an organization can understand. A business glossary ensures organizations speak the same language by clearing up ambiguity in business terminology. These definitions form part of a business ontology – helping organizations understand how different terms relate to one another.[14]

The Pivotal Role of Data Governance

The history of data governance can be traced back to various legislative, regulatory, and technological developments in the United States. According to Gartner (2024), data governance is the specification of decision rights and an accountability framework to ensure appropriate behavior in the valuation, creation, consumption, and control of data and analytics. Data governance processes and systems must be continuously updated to meet the demands of evolving legislation and to capitalize on emerging technological opportunities.

---

[13] As defined in the Harvard Business Review article "5 Principles of Data Ethics for Business", which can be found here: https://online.hbs.edu/blog/post/data-ethics.

[14] As defined by Collibra, https://www.collibra.com/blog/what-is-a-business-glossary.

Take a Moment (#2)

Does your company have a data governance framework in place, or has it ever? What kinds of project work did they do? Name a few projects/initiatives.

Here are some key legislative milestones and considerations for integrating technology shifts into effective data governance practices.

Privacy Legislation

Companies need to govern the access and use of data to manage data security and privacy while making it available for more efficient business operations. They must also adhere to privacy legislation, such as:

- The Fair Credit Reporting Act (FCRA) of 1970 establishes privacy protection for personal data;
- The Gramm-Leach-Bliley Act (GLBA) of 1999, mandates that financial institutions protect the security and confidentiality of customer information;
- The Health Insurance Portability and Accountability Act (HIPAA) of 1996, introduces standards for the use and protection of health information; and
- The Children's Online Privacy Protection Act (COPPA) of 1998 regulates the online collection of personal information from children under 13 years of age.

Technology Advancement

Internet of Things (IoT) devices, social media, and mobile devices have led to a proliferation of data, presenting challenges in managing the volume, velocity, veracity, and variety of data (known as the four Vs of big data). This proliferation is a double-edged sword: while it fuels powerful insights, enables real-time market analysis, and supports hyper-personalized consumer engagement, it also increases the risk of fragmented data ecosystems. However, data stored across multiple cloud environments raises significant concerns about data security, privacy, and compliance.

Artificial Intelligence and machine learning are increasingly critical for data governance tasks such as data classification, metadata management, and policy enforcement. At the same time, these technologies can introduce algorithmic biases that require the implementation of guardrails, ensuring transparency, and conducting regular audits to monitor for ethical implications.

Emerging global regulations, such as the EU's AI Act, are also shaping how organizations approach AI governance as part of their broader data governance strategies. In this increasingly complex environment, effective data governance must evolve to strike a balance between agility and oversight, empowering innovation while maintaining trust and compliance.

Data Governance Role Expanding in Business Strategy

Data governance is evolving beyond a legal compliance function into an enabler of business value. Gartner[15] predicts that the role of data and analytics officers is changing as organizations

---

[15] Gartner Research - article: "Over 100 data and analytics predictions through 2028."

transition to being driven by data and analytics. Data, as a result, is a core business asset. Chief data and analytics officers are increasingly expected to deliver measurable outcomes, including revenue impact and product-level accountability. With data as a critical business enabler, data governance becomes essential to ensure the organization's access to timely, high-quality, reliable, and actionable data.

Data governance provides several advantages to businesses. It ensures that trustworthy, consistent, and relevant data is available to various stakeholders, enabling more informed decision-making, strategic planning, and improved business outcomes.

As artificial intelligence takes over many analytics functions, a unified and governed data framework becomes essential. AI systems are expected to surface insights, tell data-driven stories, and recommend customer journeys and business outcomes— functions that are only as good as the underlying data quality and structure. Users must rely on high-quality data for enhanced operational efficiency.

Clear policies, roles, and responsibilities for data management facilitate data sharing and collaboration across departments. Organizations can reduce costs by eliminating data redundancies and minimizing data-related errors. The risk of data breaches and data losses is reduced with better controls and data security protocols.

A robust data governance program also supports a data-driven culture by promoting data literacy, accountability, and stewardship at all levels of the organization. When treated as a strategic asset, data can uncover hidden insights, fuel innovation, and surface new business opportunities, resulting in a meaningful competitive advantage.

A strong commitment to data governance also signals a commitment to data ethics and customer privacy - key factors in building long-term brand trust and reputational resilience.

Marriage of Data Governance and Change Leadership

"The success of a data governance initiative depends on effective organizational change management across all levels of the agency."

Diana Barrett, Data Officer (State Government)

Traditionally, we describe data governance change leadership as involving four components: People, Processes, Data, and Technology. Change management models such as Leavitt's Diamond Model[16] focus on organizational changes that transform the structure, culture, or strategies of an organization. Data governance change leadership's goal is to manage changes in how data is managed, secured, accessed and used. We are already witnessing a major shift in technology and processes within organizations that result in immense volume, velocity, and variety

---

[16] https://changemanagementinsight.com/what-is-leavitts-diamond-model/.

of data available to them. Data governance is the science of how this data is managed as an organizational asset.

One area that requires careful consideration is upskilling employees in both leveraging data to support data-centric strategies and developing their change leadership skills. A typical data governance department in an average-sized U.S. company has 10 to 25 employees. Many of them may have data governance in their job description. However, there may be many who support data governance tasks without being formally inducted into the data governance program. Formal roles such as data governance director, data steward, data quality analyst, data governance specialist, data governance architect, data privacy officer, and compliance officer may depend on the organization's level of data maturity. Many employees are taking advantage of this lack of structure to 'volunteer' for the data governance tasks. They benefit from adding another qualification to their CV and get ready for formal data governance roles. These teams are transforming and shaping the data maturity journey of organizations as they guide them from siloed departmental data to integrated and accessible enterprise-wide data. The data governance teams must influence people's attitudes and perceptions about their understanding and use of data, helping to build a culture of data sharing and collective literacy. Thus, data governance departments manage change as a core aspect of their roles.

Data governance roles are typically housed in finance, IT, or business departments. They operate as a service arm for introducing technological advancements related to data usage.

Therefore, they need to address cultural transformation as they cultivate a culture that values prudent data management for supporting data-driven decision-making. They need to motivate users to adopt and comply with data governance policies and procedures. They need to educate and bring various internal stakeholders into the fold who may be involved in processes that currently use data being standardized. They must articulate how data governance supports overall organizational goals, business objectives, and priorities. They need to embed data governance as a source of continuous improvement, developing performance metrics that trigger adjustments according to the changing business environment. Data governance managers play a central role in *leading* this transformation toward data-driven decision-making. The ANCHOR change leadership model proposed in this book caters to precisely this need of mid-level data governance managers by equipping them with the skills to manage and lead organizational change and foster data-literate, empowered teams.

Through Aakriti's years of experience managing change initiatives, both in the data space and within the nonprofit space, she has noticed that all change initiatives share a common foundation. Effective leadership is essential for change management across people, processes, data, and technology. Hence, the ANCHOR change leadership model.

The ANCHOR model supports data governance professionals in navigating these dynamics by providing a practical, repeatable framework for leading change. The ANCHOR model encapsulates six factors, with each factor addressing a core challenge of driving transformation in complex, often resource-constrained environments. It is tailored for mid-level managers who are expected to build momentum, align with stakeholders' goals, and sustain data governance adoption across the organization.

We review the ANCHOR change management model in the next chapter.

Is There a Need for a New Change Management Model?

"People don't resist change; they resist being changed."

Tiankai Feng, Data & AI Strategy Director (Consulting/Professional Services)

While there are numerous methodologies regarding change management,[17] these are not particularly suitable in the data governance space for the following reasons:

1. Many models depict employees as resistors, which isn't always the case. Generally, employees strive to improve their job performance. Change triggers feelings of fear within individuals, and managing change effectively must involve carefully managing the fear that people feel when change occurs. You can do so by having people engage in the change initiative, allowing them to

---

[17] A list of other models is available in the appendix.

participate in decision-making so they feel they have a seat at the table.

2. These models underplay the role of ethics, power, and politics. A successful change initiative must persuade people of the benefits of change. Many people make decisions based on their emotions. They often have conflicting priorities—the priorities of their job and personal career goals. If they understand that one of the benefits of change may be personal growth, then perhaps they will be more open to it.

3. Most of these models expect senior leadership to be the project sponsors. The senior leaders communicate the need for change to the rest of the organization and set targets and a clear direction. Leader communication may be critical for organizational change initiatives. That may not be the case in data governance projects, where senior leaders mostly need to understand the value of the project. The communication of the project's importance lies with the data governance leader, who then has to sell it to their peers in business departments and to their superiors.

4. As discussed earlier, many of these models presume the availability of a centralized project management office. Using a project management office means focusing on the timeline and steps; change is slow and cannot be rushed. Change is not processed linearly, as every person

experiencing change has a different appetite and speed of adoption.

5. Many models don't focus on learning from failures, but instead quickly move past them and never revisit them. As we discussed earlier, the failure rate for change initiatives is extremely high, and therefore, we must learn from these failures.

6. Many models overemphasize technology as a focus area. Laura Madsen[18] said in her book, Disrupting Data Governance,[19] "Fixing data governance is not really about technology. No technology in the world can save your data governance program from itself. Technology can't solve broken processes, lack of people, lack of knowledge of the people, or poorly defined functions." To handle change and succeed in your data governance program, you must focus on the human factors of change, not the technology.

7. Change logging is not the same as change management or change leadership. Logging the changes you make to a document may be a part of your data governance program, but we are not responsible for enforcing changes or managing documents. Change leadership is

---

[18] Youtube "[Webinar with Laura Madsen] Disruptive Data Governance that doesn't suck" by Metric Insights, https://www.youtube.com/watch?v=C-D6kdTrfxE.

[19] Disrupting Data Governance: A Call to Action, by Laura Madsen. Technics Publications, 2019.

broader than logging and involves changing minds and hearts about data governance, as well as inspiring people to get involved.

8. Many models don't appreciate incremental change. Change happens in tiny increments over time. We do ourselves a massive disservice by ignoring small changes and focusing only on big movements.

9. People often don't center their change initiative in their communication practices. A lack of communication surrounding the change leads to the downfall of the change effort because people don't feel involved and don't buy into it. Simply telling people what you're working on can have a huge impact on the success of the people side of your program.

10. Many models ignore the importance of cultural contexts and factors. Every organization has its own culture, but so does every team. Being aware of and adapting your tactics to suit the culture is critical to success.

As we continue to discuss the ANCHOR model, we'll overcome the constraints listed above and discuss how to manage these issues.

More specifically, the existing change management models were developed in response to:

1. The need for an organization-wide change, such as a change in structure, or to accommodate mergers and acquisitions. Such models represent a huge but one-time change. These models assume that a need for a strategic response drives change. Therefore, change is driven by senior managers through a centralized entity, such as a project management office. Models such as McKinsey's 7-S model, Lewin's model, and Kotter's model are examples of such models. Many of these models have been modified to be used in other situations, but were primarily developed to respond to an organization-wide, one-time change initiative.

2. The need to show that change is a slow process that may take time. Change cannot be directed, but it can be suggested. Models like the Nudge Theory and Bridge's Transition Model address change as a process.

3. The need for models that are targeted at individuals, such as the ADKAR, Kubler-Ross, and Satir models. The ADKAR model suggests that an individual must go through five stages before accepting change. These stages are: create awareness, desire, knowledge, ability, and acceptance. According to ADKAR, successful change management requires guiding each employee or concerned staff member through these five stages for change to occur.

As you may notice, there is a need for a change leadership model that applies to a mid-management team tasked with implementing change, such as a data governance team. The model needs to focus on managing people, motivating and inspiring team members, and addressing the needs of stakeholders and employees whose processes and roles may be impacted by changes in how data is accessed, stored, and made available. We introduce the ANCHOR model of change leadership.

The ANCHOR Model

The ANCHOR model is a six-factor model that you can apply to anchor your change initiative or data governance program into your organization's culture. The six factors that comprise change leadership in the data governance space are:

- **Factor 1, Aim:** Find clarity around the scope of your data governance program, gather opportunities, and prioritize your work based on the resources at your disposal.

- **Factor 2, Need:** Align your goals with your organization's goals and communicate business value to your leadership.

- **Factor 3, Community:** Find 'volunteers' across your organization that can help you achieve your goals;

engage their heads and hearts; eventually hire a team of your own.

- **Factor 4, Hooray!** Celebrate your volunteers and team members by identifying and communicating successes and making people feel appreciated.

- **Factor 5, Obstacles:** Identify barriers that are in your way, particularly organizational and cultural barriers, and work to remove them.

- **Factor 6, Resilience:** Understand what causes change initiatives to fail, and use your understanding of the ANCHOR process to overcome those issues; measure growth and build on your momentum and ensure the change initiative takes root.

Note: The Agrawal ANCHOR Model's factors do not occur in the same order every time and often repeat. They can and will occur concurrently, requiring team input and not just based on top-down policies.

CHAPTER ONE

Aim

From Fog to Focus

"Nothing changes if nothing changes."

Valerie Bonventre Calvo,
Vice President of Data Governance & Enablement (Financial Services)

41

Before leading your change, you must be clear about what you're changing. The 'Aim' is the investigative and fact-finding factor of the ANCHOR model. During 'Aim,' we lay the groundwork to clarify why a data governance department is needed. We will also identify (1) the potential project options we could pursue, and (2) decide where our limited resources are best applied for maximum impact.

As data governance professionals, managing scarce resources, including our own time and energy, is paramount to ensuring success for the organization. Data governance is a continuous program comprising many projects or lines of work. Therefore, we need to have a clear purpose for our program, listen to our clients, understand the opportunities for impact, and prioritize those opportunities into a focused set of action items.

Finding a Unified Direction for Your Program

Often, data governance programs start as a one-person department. Ask Aakriti, who started her career in data governance in an unusual way. Following an interview for a data analyst position, she was offered a role as a data governance analyst, a field she was unfamiliar with. Tasked with starting a program, she needed to determine aspects of data governance without knowing what the program's scope should or could realistically encompass.

There is little direction except that "something needs to be done about data". However, data governance must be aligned with the needs of your organization. For example, if the data management team aims to create a single database containing all information within the organization, data governance can assist by establishing metadata (a technical term that means defining data so that users can make sense of it) and standardizing that information for use across the organization. The same customer may often buy different products from your company and, therefore, be duplicated across customer databases. The metadata can link this person across the product types so that sales teams have a complete view of the customer's relationships with the organization.

Thus, understanding what is critical to the organization's success helps set the direction for the data governance team. This alignment ensures that the data governance team is not only managing data but also actively enabling the organization's strategic goals - whether that's improving customer experience, facilitating cross-sell opportunities, or supporting compliance. It's helpful to ask: What organizational pain points could be solved through better data clarity, consistency, or accountability? These questions help root your direction in real business priorities.

Defining Scope

"Data governance work is the management of chaos. You inherited chaos, and you are probably, at the moment, creating more chaos by trying to fix that previous chaos."

Diana Barrett, Data Officer (State Government)

Before deciding which data problems to solve, we must first understand the scope of our work. Data governance is, unfortunately, defined differently across different organizations. It's essential to clarify the specific scope and responsibilities of your department within your organization's structure and goals.

Take a Moment (#3)

Think about the following questions:

Why is a data governance program being initiated, or re-evaluated, at this time?
Was it a mandate from leadership?
Was it a response to compliance or regulatory pressure?
Was it intended to help fix business inefficiencies or errors?
Was it to create better reporting or analytics?
Other?

Who initiated the conversation about data governance?
Executive sponsor
Data team
IT department
Business unit
Other

What do people in your organization believe "data governance" means? Include a few diverse stakeholder perspectives.

Depending on your organization, you may oversee or manage some or many of the following tasks:

- Creating and managing a metadata repository or business glossary
- Defining and implementing data quality rules within databases
- Managing sensitive data based on regulatory requirements and the needs of the business
- Creating and socializing a data literacy program
- Applying data security procedures and ensuring access control
- Ensuring compliance with data-related regulations, such as GDPR or HIPAA
- Implementing policies for data retention, deletion, and lifecycle management
- Assessing and mitigating any data-related risks
- Conducting data management training for other employees of the organization
- Writing and/or implementing policies related to data governance, data management, or any of the tasks listed above

Not all data governance departments will handle every function listed here, but understanding your team's charter helps clarify priorities and boundaries.

Take a Moment (#4)

Create a list of what your data governance program encompasses. Which tasks from the list above are part of your purview, and which aren't? What other tasks are you expected to oversee and manage?

Now that you know what tasks to include within your data governance program, develop a mission and vision statement for your program. These statements will communicate the purpose of your department's existence and could serve as an elevator pitch to encourage people to help with your work and achieve your mission.

Mission and Vision Statements

Mission statements are clear sentences that state what your department is offering, to whom, and why you're doing it. They also define how your department is distinct from others and where it adds unique value. It's generally written in the present tense, as it is what you're working on currently.[20]

Vision statements, on the other hand, are more idealistic or aspirational. They tend to be ambitious, future-focused, and describe your department's long-term impact. They serve as the north star for your team, defining what an ideal state will look like once you've completed all of the work that data governance is meant to do. Vision statements are typically written in the future tense to reflect the desired end state.

Examples of mission and vision statements for data governance departments are provided below. Tailor yours to be as personalized as you would like. Keep in mind that you want to use these statements to communicate the scope of work for your team, so be specific and use the list from the activity above.

When well-crafted, these statements not only guide your team internally, they also serve as tools for communicating your purpose and focus to leadership, stakeholders, and collaborators.

---

[20] Resource: Mission and Vision Statements (Hubspot Blog, Inspiring Company Mission Statements) https://blog.hubspot.com/marketing/inspiring-company-mission-statements.

Sample Mission and Vision Statements
Scope of work: Metadata management and data quality

- **Mission statement:** To empower our colleagues to make better data-driven decisions by ensuring the understanding and integrity of our corporation's data. We aim to cultivate a data-centric culture by promoting cross-functional knowledge of data assets and fostering trust in the data being used, enabling our colleagues to confidently self-serve.

- **Vision statement:** Our vision is to become the enterprise-wide hub for reliable, high-quality data, where every colleague can access, understand, and act on information with confidence.

Scope of work: Data Privacy and Regulatory Compliance (e.g., GDPR, HIPAA)

- **Mission statement:** To safeguard our organization's data by implementing policies, practices, and controls that ensure privacy, security, and compliance with applicable regulations. We empower teams to handle sensitive data responsibly while minimizing risk and protecting individual rights.

- **Vision statement:** To build an organization where data privacy is embedded in every business process, compliance is proactive, and trust is foundational to our data practices.

Scope of Work: Data Access and Security Controls

- **Mission statement:** To create a secure, permission-based data ecosystem that enables innovation without compromising confidentiality, integrity, or regulatory compliance.
- **Vision statement:** To ensure the right people have access to the right data at the right time, securely and efficiently, by establishing clear access protocols and scalable data security standards.

Scope of Work: Data Literacy and Culture Enablement

- **Mission statement:** To elevate the organization's data literacy by providing accessible resources, education, and support that enable all employees to confidently engage with data in their daily work.
- **Vision statement:** To create a culture where every employee understands the value of data, speaks a shared data language, and actively participates in data-driven decision-making.

Scope of Work: Full-Scope Enterprise Data Governance (Cross-functional + Strategic)

- **Mission statement:** To define, implement, and steward enterprise data governance policies and practices that ensure data is accurate, accessible, secure, and aligned with business strategy.
- **Vision statement:** To transform the organization into a data-first enterprise where information is governed as a strategic asset, driving innovation, operational excellence, and competitive advantage.

Take a Moment (#5)

Write your own mission and vision statements for your Data Governance program.

Gathering Opportunities

Now that we understand the scope of work for our data governance program, we need to determine which projects to focus on. To do this, we need to listen carefully to people within our organizations whom we may be able to help through the data governance program.

We recommend a tool for this factor called 'Data Therapy.' Here is how Data Therapy works:

Data Therapy

One of the best ways to learn about your client's needs is to ask! "Data Therapy" can be an effective and efficient way to do this. Data Therapy is a free-flowing, one-on-one conversation—like a therapy session —where you act as the listener and guide, and your client shares their data-related frustrations, challenges, and workflows. During data therapy, we ask our clients to discuss their data-related woes and problems to better understand where we can assist them.

Identify 5-10 individuals within your organization whom you consider potential clients. Preferably, these folks are both hands-on with data and embedded in high-impact business areas. A successful Data Therapy session requires the data governance team to build trust with these users.

A typical Data Therapy session lasts approximately 40-50 minutes. Avoid longer meetings, as they may be less productive. Multiple sessions may be necessary to fully identify the range of challenges and pain points. Sometimes, you may need to schedule separate meetings with different groups of employees within the relevant department. They may have different needs, and perhaps some may not be well-prepared or open with their requirements. They may be following a process that is traditionally followed in their department without questioning it. As the saying goes, "Why fix what isn't broken?"—but this mindset often hides inefficiencies and opportunities for improvement.

The goal of Data Therapy is not to diagnose or "fix" immediately but to listen empathetically, document themes, and begin spotting areas where governance can create value.

Data Therapy Session Guide

Purpose: To build trust with stakeholders, uncover data challenges, and identify opportunities where the data governance team can provide value.

Session Length: 40–50 minutes

Participants:
- 1–2 data governance team members (listeners)
- 1 stakeholder or small group from a department that uses or manages data

Preparation:

- Identify 5–10 stakeholders who are close to the data and tied to key business goals
- Schedule 1:1 or small-group conversations
- Bring a notetaking template or whiteboard tool (feel free to use the one included below)
- Let the participant know that this is an informal and exploratory session, not a technical audit. Additionally, emphasize confidentiality and refrain from recording the session. Mention that you will not be able to resolve all data issues, but you will do your best to assist in any way possible.

Tone to Set:

- Conversational, empathetic, and non-judgmental
- Your job is to listen, not fix in the moment
- Build rapport and curiosity

Sample Questions for a Data Therapy Session

During your session, ask your client about their data issues. Below is a list of sample questions you may want to ask. Don't forget that, at times, once you receive an answer to a question, you may need to dig deeper. This is how you can identify the root cause of the issue.

General Discovery:

- "Can you walk me through a day in your role? How do you use data?"

- "What are some of the most important reports or datasets you rely on?"
- "How confident do you feel in the data you're using?"

Data Quality and Trust:
- "Are there any reports or dashboards you don't fully trust? Why?"
- "Do you often have to clean or manipulate data manually? What does that process look like?"
- "Have you ever found inconsistent or conflicting data in different systems?"

Access and Control:
- "Do you always have access to the data you need?"
- "Are there datasets you wish you had but can't get to?"
- "Do you ever worry about who else has access to sensitive data?"

Metadata and Understanding:
- "Is it always clear to you what a column or data field means?"
- "Have you ever had to guess what something in a report represented?"
- "Do you have a central place to find definitions, or do you rely on asking colleagues?"

Analytics and Outcomes:
- "How is data used in decision-making in your team or department?"

- "Do you feel leadership understands or values the data work being done?"
- "What would make data more useful in your job?"

Processes and Culture:

- "What's a data-related process that's always frustrated you?"
- "Are there outdated habits or workarounds your team still follows?"
- "What's one thing you wish you could change about how your department uses data?"

For all of the questions above, you may use some of the following questions to probe for more details, dig deeper into the root cause, or help determine business value:

To dig into the Root Cause:

- "Can you walk me step-by-step through what happens when this issue comes up?"
- "When did you first notice this problem? Has it always been this way?"
- "Is this an isolated issue, or do you see it in other areas too?"
- "What do you think is causing this? Have you tried to fix it before?"
- "Who else touches this data before or after you?"
- "Where is the breakdown happening—in the system, the process, or communication?"
- "If you had perfect data, would this problem still exist?"

To Understand the Business Impact:

- "How does this issue affect your ability to do your job?"
- "What happens downstream if this data is wrong or delayed?"
- "How does this impact your customers, clients, or partners?"
- "Do you or your team spend extra time working around this problem? How much?"
- "Have there ever been mistakes, delays, or decisions made because of this?"
- "If we could fix this, what would that unlock for you or your team?"

To Determine the Business Value or Priority:

- "If we were to prioritize this issue, what would be the biggest benefit to the business?"
- "Who else would benefit from this being fixed or improved?"
- "Would this save money and time, or reduce risk? Can you estimate how much?"
- "If we had to rank this against other challenges, where would it fall?"
- "Is this something leadership cares about, or is tracking today?"
- "Are there metrics we could use to measure improvement here?"

Post-Data Therapy Session Tips

Don't jump to solutioning—focus on hearing and analyzing what was said.

Identify:

- quick wins
- strategic initiatives
- structural challenges or policy needs.

Consider summarizing key takeaways in a short email back to the participant to build trust and show that you heard them. Check if they have any other observations that they may like to add.

Caution!

Only the therapist and client(s) should speak. It's fine to invite additional team members to listen in, as long as your client is comfortable with it. Make sure there is no conflict of interest, particularly if the listeners are in the same reporting chain as the client. Ensure that none of your listeners speaks. They are like flies on the wall—silent observers only.

Do not record your session. In a hybrid or virtual environment where recordings are common, resist the urge to hit 'record.' Assign one of your silent listeners to be a notetaker—or take notes yourself—but do not record the session. Recording will put your clients on edge, and they may fear transparency and backlash for being vulnerable or honest. Trust is paramount. Emphasize that anything said in this room stays in the room, and ensure all listeners keep the secret and respect that confidentiality.

Do not problem-solve during the session. This is a listening session. Your goal is to listen deeply, uncover core challenges, and only later begin to explore solutions. Ask questions to get to the root issues and keep trying to dig deeper.

If you feel like your organization is not ready for "therapy," remember that you can do this without calling it therapy. Invite people to a "coffee chat", a "one-on-one", an "information session", a "get to know you session", a "touch base", or whatever terminology is prevalent within your organization. What matters most is creating a safe space where people feel heard, regardless of what you call it.

Quick reference reminders for building psychological safety:
- Ask for permission before inviting others
- Reinforce confidentiality
- Always follow up with gratitude.

Data Therapy in Practice—A Case Study

Alejandra works for a company based in Colombia, where she is a Data Governance Manager, trying to start a data governance program from scratch, but she didn't know where to start. After learning about Data Therapy, Alejandra felt this could be a method to explore different alternatives and find quick wins.

"As data people, we're writing data strategy, but at the end of the day, are we being objective? We are basing our strategy purely on our feelings and assumptions. We need to talk to our internal stakeholders. I proposed data therapy. I worked with marketing to make a zen data therapy logo, to create a peaceful environment for our clients. I put together a few questions—because I wanted a guide, but wanted to also make sure the conversation wasn't heavily scripted and flowed.

"I started to book meetings with people across the company—C-levels to seniors, to directors to mid-levels, to a few analysts. I wanted varied perspectives from across the enterprise. I invited them to Data Therapy, and didn't provide too many details on the sessions beforehand—I didn't want them to be overly prepared.

"I put coffee out, put up signage saying "Data Therapy Do Not Disturb". I wanted my clients to be in the correct mindset. At the beginning of each session, I introduced myself—"My name is Alejandra, I am the data governance manager. Have you heard of data governance?" This was a good method for me to tell them about our department if they hadn't heard. Then, I would tell them that this is a confidential space, and that anything they say will be kept between us. I then said that I couldn't promise that I can solve their problems now, or even a year from now, but I promise that we'll be adding it to the roadmap.

"Then I would say, I'm your therapist—and you are my client with data trauma. I told them that this is not a letter to Santa—I want them to focus on their top two or three issues. Most people were ready to tell me their problems; they were not hesitant.

"Data therapy sessions allowed me to create a relationship with my stakeholders, and also emphasized that I want to see their mess under the carpet. I used all of the issues I gathered from data therapy sessions and then did my own prioritization.

"After this initial usage of data therapy, I continued to conduct these sessions in my organization. At my next organization, I was tasked with building a data literacy program, so I used data therapy again during my research phase. I interviewed stakeholders to figure out what kind of topics they would want to learn, and came up with different paths for different types of folks—technical and non-technical. Allowing people to have input allowed them to feel like they were part of the solution. Bringing them in early helped create a stronger relationship and more buy-in for our data literacy program once released."

Quotes from interview with Maria Alejandra Restrepo, Data Governance Manager (Technology)

Data Therapy
Session Notes

© 2020, THE ANCHOR MODEL,
AAKRITI AGRAWAL & ARVIND AGRAWAL

Date and Time	Department	Topic/Objectives

Attendees

Client

Therapist

Listeners

Notes

Issue 1

Description

Impact/Business Value

Possible Solutions

Issue 2

Description

Impact/Business Value

Possible Solutions

Key Learnings

Followups/Next Steps

Can be downloaded from: AnchorYourChange.com.

Prioritizing Opportunities

Now that you've heard what opportunities may exist for you to work on, it's important to decide on the best place to start! Remember, as a data governance professional starting a new program, not only do you often not have a team of your own yet, but you may also be balancing your data governance responsibilities with other tasks. You must evaluate your available capacity, time, skills, and the extent of your access to stakeholders to identify which projects offer the greatest return on your limited resources. There are several ways to conduct this evaluation, which we'll discuss next.

Note: this isn't just about picking the 'biggest' problem - it's about selecting the initiative that builds momentum, earns trust, and demonstrates early value.

Ways of Choosing the Most Critical Data to Govern

You may choose to prioritize your projects for data governance based on the criticality or business value of the data itself. Every organization does this differently, but we'd like to share four of the most common approaches: the Domain approach, the Regulatory approach, the Risk approach, and the Usability approach. You may choose the mechanism that best suits your organization.

The Domain Approach:

As the name suggests, data governance projects are chosen from a specific business domain, since business domains may have unique data needs and challenges. This requires tailoring governance efforts to meet domain-specific priorities. Choosing a domain may depend on the priority set by the organization or the criticality of the challenge your organization faces. You may need to establish specific policies and processes related to the chosen domain, develop solutions for domain-specific issues, and set up KPIs relevant to that domain.

Since you are developing a program for a specific domain, you can enhance their operational efficiency and strengthen their decision-making capabilities. Improving the availability and quality of domain-specific data may create a strategic advantage.

There may be some consequences to taking on domain-specific projects. For example, you may develop metadata and standards to meet the unique needs of one domain while unintentionally disregarding the needs of others. This could result in conflicting definitions, duplicate work, or the need to revisit decisions later.

Example: Finance and Marketing may both store sales data, but for different purposes.

- Finance may only keep records related to paid incentives to ensure accurate accounting.
- Marketing may track all sales data, including unpaid or ineligible incentive transactions.

Thus, the two teams could define "sales" differently, leading to conflicting data sets.

This example illustrates the importance of cross-domain coordination, even when executing domain-specific governance efforts.

The Regulatory Approach:

This approach focuses on adhering to applicable laws, policies, and compliance requirements. Projects prioritized under this model are those that ensure compliance with data privacy, usage, storage, and protection regulations.

Examples include:

- Consent collection and documentation (e.g., for customer or vendor data)
- Mapping regulatory requirements across jurisdictions
- Creating policies for access control and data usage.

In such a case, business needs may take a back seat when prioritizing compliance deadlines. In such cases, compliance timelines may take precedence over other business needs.

You may also need to:

- Train employees on security and privacy practices
- Conduct regular audits to ensure internal adherence to regulations
- Involve front-line employees who handle sensitive data.

Benefits: Mitigating legal and reputational risk, maintaining stakeholder trust, and demonstrating accountability. Caution: Data built solely for regulatory reporting may not be suitable for business intelligence or strategic use, so ensure that standards serve multiple purposes whenever possible.

The Risk Approach:

This approach prioritizes efforts based on the potential risk associated with data use, access, or loss. Risks may include:

- Data breaches or leaks
- Unauthorized access
- Inaccurate data leading to poor decision-making
- Privacy violations.

Governance activities may include:

- Data access controls
- Data masking and encryption
- Ongoing monitoring of key risk indicators
- Conducting risk assessments and scenario planning.

Risk mitigation should be embedded into ongoing governance improvements.

Example: The 2013 Target data breach[21] led to massive fines, technology overhauls, third-party audits, and the establishment of

---

[21] Learn more about takeaways from the 2013 Target Data Breach Incident here: https://www.cardconnect.com/launchpointe/payment-trends/target-data-breach.

an internal data security division. This illustrates how risk-based governance can prevent costly reactive measures and enable proactive resilience.

The Usability Approach:

This approach prioritizes data governance based on user experience and accessibility. Focus areas include:

- Ensuring end users (e.g., analysts, decision-makers, IT staff) can easily find and use data
- Creating user-friendly tools and documentation
- Gathering continuous feedback on data pain points
- Involving users in defining current and future needs

Governance under this model emphasizes simplicity, clarity, and training, making sure users are confident and capable of working with governed data.

Limitation: Although this approach enhances user adoption, it must still strike a balance between compliance and security. Ease of use should never compromise privacy or regulatory requirements.

Summary:

In addition to the four approaches above, you may choose projects that are:

- Time-sensitive
- Driven by executive request
- Backed by a compelling business case.

Keep in mind that these approaches may occasionally conflict—for example, usability and compliance may have competing priorities. Assessing the business case behind each option can help clarify which project should come first.

You might have noticed that every technique involves changing current processes, standards, or data protocols. That change will impact stakeholders, and getting their buy-in is critical. The ultimate challenge is managing and motivating stakeholders to support these efforts, contribute their perspectives, and adopt the changes being introduced.

Choosing the right starting point is only half the battle—gaining alignment and momentum across your organization is what determines success.

Identify Strengths Within Your Organization

Change is always difficult. Data governance aims to strengthen the organization by developing processes that ensure compliance with laws, enhance data transparency, and facilitate ethical business practices. Therefore, data governance plays a significant role in contributing to an organization that earns stakeholder trust. However, understanding the organizational culture is essential for making effective changes. Ask yourself: What do we do well? What do we struggle with? Where is there room for growth? Understanding the landscape of your organization can go a long way in ensuring a successful change.

Organizational culture refers to the shared values, beliefs, norms, customs, and behaviors that characterize an organization. An organization's culture dictates how employees interact with each other and make decisions. It's often described as the unwritten rules governing the organization's functions.

To understand the organization's culture, observe how newcomers are onboarded and socialized. If a formal process familiarizes them with various functions and introduces them to people in different departments, this may suggest a collaborative culture. Observe how leadership behaves and communicates. Leadership sets the tone for an open culture through transparency. Observe how employees interact, collaborate, and solve problems. If employees are empathetic toward each other, you have a culture where people are willing to compromise. Listen to the stories, narratives, and myths circulating within the organization. If you notice the emphasis on rules, procedures, and hierarchy, your organization may have a bureaucratic culture. This often reflects a formalized structure and centralized decision-making.

Understanding the culture can inform your communication strategy and help you prioritize which projects to tackle first. Sometimes, you may need to resolve conflicts. We discuss conflict resolution in Chapter 5 of this book.

Evaluate Effort and Impact

To prioritize your efforts, it's helpful to consider the amount of effort a project requires and the potential impact it's likely to have. The goal is to focus on projects that offer the highest return on investment—those that provide meaningful impact without overextending your team or budget.

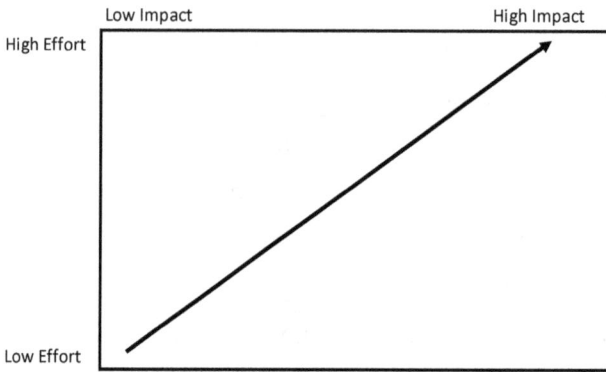

	Low Impact	High Impact
High Effort		
Low Effort		

Using the chart above, map out how much effort and impact you expect a project to have. Choose projects where you can increase the impact of your project while reducing the effort/spend.

	Low Impact	High Impact
High Effort	✓ Prioritize Immediately	🚧 Consider if Resources Allow
Low Effort	⟳ Reasess or Automate	✗ Avoid for Now

Better Manage Your To-Do Lists

Instead of making one long to-do list of everything you need to get done to make your program successful, split up your list into four lists:[22]

- A "**Do It**" list of items that are Urgent and Important: Items with a clear deadline and direct consequences if they're not completed.
- A "**Schedule It**" List of items that are Not Urgent but are Important: Items without a set deadline, but are important to bring you closer to your goals.
- A "**Delegate It**" List of Items that are Not Important but are Urgent: Items that need to be done, but don't require your specific skills, or maybe things that you don't have the skills for.
- A "**Delete It**" List of items that are neither Important nor Urgent: Items that distract you from your goal, and are possibly okay, but only in moderation.

Doing this allows us to see that not everything is a priority and can make it easier to prioritize truly important items. For example, let's say you're beginning to write a book:

---

[22] Learn more about the Eisenhower Method of Todo lists here: https://todoist.com/productivity-methods/eisenhower-matrix.

	Urgent	Not Urgent
Important	**DO IT** Items with a clear deadline and direct consequences if they're not completed Examples: • Writing the content • Deciding which chapters should be in the book • Conducting interviews to gather quotes	**SCHEDULE IT** Items without a set deadline but are important to bring you closer to your goals. Examples: • Figuring out a marketing strategy for the book • Planning a book tour
Not Important	**DELEGATE IT** Items that need to be done, but don't require your specific skills, or maybe things that you don't have the skills for Examples: • Illustrations • Designing the book cover • Titling the book	**DELETE IT** Items that distract you from your goal, and are possibly okay, but only in moderation. Examples: • Watch a movie • Scroll social media

CHAPTER TWO

Need

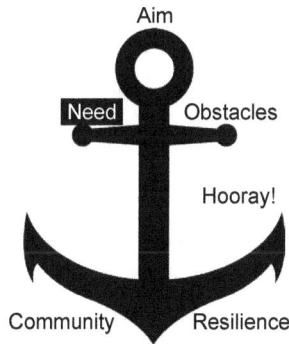

Digging for the Governance Goldmine

"There comes a point in a company when data governance is needed and embraced. There are other times when data governance is needed, but it won't be readily embraced. It takes a catalyst for change to bring data governance to the forefront and implement it effectively. When the company is ready, you must seize the opportunity as a data governance leader. You can't shy away from it and get wrapped up in the war wounds of five years ago, of things you tried to do and didn't work - you embrace it and take that opportunity and run with it."

David Smith, Data Governance Director (Footwear/Apparel)

Now that you know the areas in which you could be working, you need to ensure that the chosen path aligns with what your leadership cares about. As middle management, we find ourselves in a challenging position, managing upwards - the leadership, laterally across peers, and downward to individual contributors. However, getting funding and resources relies on our ability to advocate for our initiatives to senior leadership. This factor of the ANCHOR model, "Need", focuses on leading upwards. During 'Need,' we capitalize on the opportunities identified during the 'Aim' factor and align them with organizational priorities.

Understanding the organization's strategic goals—and clearly demonstrating how your data governance work supports them—will increase your chances of securing resources, sponsorship, and support. To maximize this, we need to articulate the business value of data governance in concrete terms. This includes estimating the return on investment, quantifying potential savings or risk reduction, and presenting these insights in a language that leadership understands.

Finding the business value and developing a business case will help shift the image of the data governance department from a cost center to a strategic business enabler. Ask yourself: What keeps our executives up at night—and how can good data mitigate that risk or unlock that opportunity?

"As a middle manager, you can be an expert or an SME in your data in your domain, but that's not enough. Right. You can manage a project and you can know exactly what you want to do and be very, very good at what you do. But you've got to manage the other stakeholders and make sure that you know everyone's voice is heard and decisions are being made. And ultimately, I think that comes down to decisions being made. As middle managers, somebody has to take that step of okay, well, who's making the decision? Because a lot of people have input, and they share analysis. So even as middle manager like myself, whenever I come into a project I'm looking for that project leader, or the project manager. We're looking at who's going to keep us honest to our timeline. And if we don't have someone that can take that role, then I'll volunteer myself."

John (Hyun Ki) Lee, Associate Director of Data Governance (Financial Services)

Align with Organizational Priorities

To align yourself with organizational priorities, you must first identify your organization's top strategic goals. Start by doing some research. Pay attention to what your leader - or leaders above them - are talking about. What are their key performance indicators (KPIs)? What are they being held accountable for this year? Look for overlaps between those goals and the issues uncovered during your Data Therapy sessions discussed on page 52. Can data governance play a role in helping solve one of their top priorities? The closer your proposed work is to what leadership already cares about, the easier it will be to gain approval, funding, and long-term support.

Take a Moment (#6)

Make a list of your organization's priorities or goals. Are any of these areas where you could do some data governance work?

A significant part of understanding organizational priorities is also determining what drives your data governance program in the first place - whether those drivers are internal or external. Understanding the motivation and context behind the program's launch may help determine the change leadership strategies you need to apply.

"Change is all around us all the time, and it's driven both by external and internal factors. I would say it's a rarity when there is no change."

Tiankai Feng, Data & AI Strategy Director (Consulting/Professional Services)

If your data governance program is being motivated by external factors, it may be driven by:

- **Regulation**: Organizations must comply with evolving regulations related to privacy, healthcare, finance, and cybersecurity. For example, BASEL III, a financial regulation, requires a certain level of capital adequacy ratio. While this begins as an external mandate, compliance efforts often evolve into internal capabilities, such as improved risk prediction, which become lasting institutional assets. In addition, the data used to calculate the capital adequacy ratio may fall under data governance to ensure it is of high quality.

- **Data protection frameworks**: Frameworks such as the EU-US Privacy Shield, APEC Cross-Border Privacy Rules, and other international agreements may dictate rules for data access, use, and processing. Since rules vary by country, you need to build a system that is flexible enough to accommodate different legal requirements. You may also need to consult with legal counsel or local compliance teams to monitor country-specific obligations.

- **Globalization and data localization requirements**: Global organizations must comply with local regulations that govern where data can be stored and processed. This means you may need to customize your systems and workflows to align with data sovereignty requirements in each country where you operate. Be vigilant about evolving laws, and continuously update your knowledge of relevant legislation. Make friends with the legal team at your organization. They can be your eyes and ears about data-related regulation. In case the legal team is not tracking data-related regulations, you need to educate them about the importance of complying with data-related laws.

- **Third-party relationships:** When organizations share data with vendors, suppliers, or other third parties, governance becomes essential to ensure data standardization and mitigate risks. Third-party vendors must also comply with relevant regulations and meet your organization's data privacy and security expectations. They must implement systems capable of handling, protecting, and interpreting the data they exchange with you. Since some third-party processors serve multiple clients, you may need to audit their practices to confirm alignment with your standards.

Internal factors are those within your company that may have caused your data governance program to start, including:

- **Organizational structure:** The structure of your organization—such as departmental silos or hierarchical models—influences how data is created, accessed, and shared. Creating a common vocabulary across the company may be your goal, enabling access to such data across the organization while maintaining its security. However, this can be challenging, particularly when persuading departments to make their data accessible. Use the skills that you learned earlier about reading your organization's culture to build relationships with various stakeholders. It helps to frame data sharing as a mutual benefit—departments may relinquish some control. Still, they also gain access to higher-quality, more consistent data and greater alignment with enterprise goals. In any case, they are working towards the organization's goal of compliance with the regulation.

- **Improved Decision-Making**: A desire to enable better decision-making and increase data accessibility may have motivated the launch of your governance program. **This is a strong motivator—improved decisions can lead to increased revenue, competitive advantage, and organizational agility. If this is the case, leadership**

may already support the program, which positions you well to resolve conflicts quickly and demonstrate results. Note: Many data governance programs may start as a reaction to external factors, but ultimately evolve into providing enhanced decision-making capability. Therefore, be alert to the evolving needs that your project may trigger.

- **Data Quality Issues**: Recurring issues with data quality may have prompted leadership to initiate a governance program. In this case, it's essential to investigate why these issues occurred in the first place. Understanding the impact of poor data quality and root causes will help you prioritize fixes, build credibility, and ensure the success of your program.

Your program may be motivated by a combination of internal and external factors, but understanding the initial catalyst is helpful as you work to align your efforts with leadership priorities and position your program for long-term support.

Convey Business Value

"Everytime you introduce something new, unless it's in people's job description, they're probably rightfully going to see it as an added task that they will have to do. A lot of times, people either don't get good buy-in, or don't understand how the work is going to contribute to their work, their team's work, or the agency. They just write it off—they just want to be left alone once the project is over."

Diana Barrett, Data Officer (State Government), on the importance of conveying value.

Take a Moment (#7)

Now that you have this extra layer of information, look back at your list from Chapter 1 - Aim and see if the priority for what to work on has changed. Write your thoughts here:

Corporations talk in terms of dollars and cents, especially the for-profit variety. That means you need to speak that language too! Even the non-profits need to ascertain whether they are making sound investments.

Conveying the value of your project - even when estimated or based on assumptions - is essential to support your long-term success. By articulating tangible benefits that your data governance project can deliver, stakeholders can better understand how it supports organizational growth and strategic goals. This allows leadership to advocate for data governance and enables you to gain resources, whether in time, funding, executive attention, or dedicated staff, that might otherwise be unavailable.

There are four primary methods for conveying business value to your stakeholders. You may use a combination of these methods to convey business value.

Method 1: Focus on Financial Incentives

This method focuses on the program's value in dollars and cents. What measurable financial value can you demonstrate through improved data governance? Are you saving time by cleaning the data? Can you estimate how much time or cost is saved through cleaner, more accurate data? Perhaps decisions are more accurate. Are there duplicative or manual processes that your program has eliminated?

That may mean saving time as well as faster decisions. Does centralizing data through a common dictionary or metadata layer enable more robust reporting and smarter decision-making? Does access to data allow people to think of innovative ways to tackle an issue?

It might be helpful to estimate the amount of time you're saving for employees and multiply that by the number of people working in that area of your company. You can use publicly available resources, like the U.S. Bureau of Labor Statistics salary data, to estimate the value of time saved.

It's also important to be conservative in your estimates and document your assumptions. Remember to underestimate your numbers and clearly state your assumptions. Underestimating builds credibility—your leadership is less likely to challenge your case, and even conservative numbers may demonstrate compelling value.

For example, through our data governance initiative and data quality efforts, we aim to reduce the time employees spend verifying client phone numbers by cleaning this data at the source. It is estimated that an analyst spends 4 hours a month cleaning this data, and 200 analysts are doing this type of work across the enterprise.

This equates to 4 hours * 12 months * 200 analysts = 9,600 hours saved annually. Assuming that an analyst receives $62,000 annually, we can determine that this equates to $29.80 per hour.

Saving 9,600 hours of work per year equals saving $286,080 annually.

In this example, we can see that using base numbers and underestimating still yields a significant amount of value that we can present to leadership. You can also present savings over multiple years or calculate the Return on Investment (ROI) by comparing savings to the cost of your program.

Method 2: Focus on Qualitative Value

Not all data governance values are in dollars and cents. It's also important to convey other types of value, such as improving the day-to-day work experience for your colleagues or clients. What kind of inefficiencies do they face daily, and how does your data governance department improve things for them? Does your work reduce frustration, eliminate manual tasks, or streamline collaboration? Consider the effects of perception from dissatisfied customers, business partners, and bad publicity.

This may help employees deliver higher-quality work, make better decisions, and feel more empowered in their roles. These kinds of benefits can be difficult to quantify in dollars, but they're still valuable—and they're worth communicating.

Share stories and examples of how data governance has made people's jobs easier, helped teams work together more effectively, or supported a healthier data culture. You might use testimonials, before-and-after process visuals, or feedback from Data Therapy sessions (with permission, of course) to highlight these softer benefits.

Method 3: Focus on Security or Risk Aversion

Bad data has a high cost, especially when regulators are involved! Estimate the potential financial impact of risks such as data breaches, regulatory fines, audit findings, or non-compliance penalties.

This is a powerful method, primarily focused on cost avoidance, one of the most persuasive value drivers in risk-averse environments. You can use recent industry news or similar companies' experiences as a baseline for your assumptions. To strengthen this argument, consider highlighting the long-term reputational damage that a breach or fine could cause. A hit to customer trust or brand reputation often leads to lost sales, weakened loyalty, and negative media coverage—costs that extend far beyond the initial fine.

Method 4: Focus on Differentiation

Effective data governance leads to improved analytics and informed decision-making. That, in turn, helps your organization differentiate itself from the competition. Start by speaking with teams who manage Customer Relationship Management (CRM) systems. They may already be measuring the impact of clean, integrated customer data and can offer insights or metrics that reinforce your value. While they may focus only on customer data, your mandate is broader—governing data across the entire enterprise.[23]

Example: Spotify's competitive advantage from its data

Spotify began with a mission to combat music piracy and ensure artists were paid fairly for their work. While multiple strategies contributed to their success, including their freemium model (free streaming supported by ads) and advanced global streaming technology, one of their biggest differentiators was how they utilized data.

Spotify leveraged user data to develop unique, personalized listening experiences. They tracked listening habits and used that data to offer curated recommendations, playlists, genres, and artist suggestions. This innovation gave them a distinct edge over competitors like Apple Music, Amazon Music, and Pandora.

Some notable data-powered features include:

- **Discover Weekly**: A playlist personalized for each user based on their listening patterns

---

[23] For additional details and techniques for business impact, please reference Executing Data Quality Projects: Ten Steps to Quality Data and Trusted Information ™, 2nd Ed (2021, Elsevier/Academic Press) by Danette McGilvray. Step 3 - Assess Business Impacts. While this book is focused on data quality, the qualitative and quantitative techniques apply equally well to data quality and to data governance.

- **Daily Mixes**: Blends of users' favorite tracks and new finds

- **Release Radar**: Highlights new music from artists a user follows.

Spotify's use of data and artificial intelligence allowed it to create a dynamic, engaging experience that set it apart from the competition and built customer loyalty. You can apply this same logic internally. How could better data help your organization move faster, make bolder decisions, or serve customers more uniquely than competitors?

So What's Next?

Once you know where you're headed, it's essential to develop a clear and actionable data governance strategy to maintain your momentum. A helpful resource that explains not only the "what" of a data strategy but also the "why" and the "how" is Marilu Lopez's book, Data Strategies for Data Governance.[24] This is a practical guide that explores the strategic thinking behind effective governance. In the next chapter, we'll explore how to engage people from across your organization to support and sustain your data governance program.

---

[24] *Data Strategies for Data Governance*, by Marilu Lopez (2023, Technics Publications).

CHAPTER THREE

Community

From Me to We, Building Your Data Village

Over the past decade, there has been a boom in data governance. As a result, many professionals have found themselves stepping into data governance roles—sometimes by choice, but often by being 'voluntold'—with limited guidance or formal training.

You may have entered data governance from a related field, such as data analysis, software development, or project management, or from a less traditional background, like legal, compliance, or human resources. You may also be working with others who continue in their primary roles while supporting data governance in their spare time.

In this factor of the ANCHOR model, we work on building community. Since many data governance teams start as a one-person department, or fewer, with no full-time allocation, you'll likely need to rely on 'volunteers' or colleagues from other departments who aren't formally resourced to help, but who can play an important role. People volunteer when they are curious about a role or series of tasks, but either themselves or their company may not be ready to take it on a full-time basis. This hesitancy may derive from a lack of funding to pay for a full-time or even part-time role or from an initial lack of buy-in into the program from leadership. Volunteers are open to learning new things. So keep a special eye for them. Keep this in mind: you don't need an official team to start building a coalition. Engaged peers can still contribute meaningfully, even if data governance isn't yet in their job description. We'll explore how to involve these colleagues, keep them engaged, and advocate for incorporating governance responsibilities into their roles over time.

During 'Community,' we'll also cover how to:

- Build champions
- Structure your data governance department and councils

- Secure small wins that justify growth
- Advocate for future headcount and build your dedicated team.

Who to Involve

"Data governance feels like a sales job a lot of the time because you have to not only convince people that their time and resource investment right now is going to be beneficial in three years, but need to make them see it themselves and truly believe it."

Diana Barrett, Data Officer (State Government)

Spill The Tea!

To succeed in data governance work, it is essential to collect information from people across your organization. 'Spill The Tea,' or 'Give Me The Scoop,' or 'What's the Buzz?' refers to getting information through informal chats. This is especially important if you're in a middle management role, where influence must flow in all directions.

You need to build advocates for data governance:

- Above you, to help secure resources and executive backing;
- Below you, to help you surface data challenges and implement changes;
- And alongside you, to help drive coordination and reinforce momentum across departments.

You may be asking: Who is a good champion for my data governance program?

Change adoption often follows Rogers' Law of Diffusion of Innovation Curve,[25] which tells us that some people are naturally inclined to adopt new behaviors earlier than others. Early adopters fundamentally differ from later ones, and identifying them is key.

The champions often share a few defining traits:

- They have the willingness and ability to take risks. Trying something new comes with risks, particularly the risk of failure. Early adopters tend to accept and even embrace that.
- They enjoy leadership roles and tend to be natural leaders. They are willing to step out and be 'the first' even when others are hesitant.
- They are comfortable with ambiguity. These individuals value action over certainty. They don't wait for perfect clarity; they're okay moving forward with a strong hypothesis instead of all the answers.
- They are curious and eager to learn. They ask thoughtful questions, get excited about new ideas, and bring optimism to uncertainty.
- Do you know of any individuals within your organization who might be a good fit? Let's make a list!

---

[25] https://sphweb.bumc.bu.edu/otlt/mph-modules/sb/behavioralchangetheories/behavioralchangetheories4.html.

Take a Moment (#8)

In the space below, draw a giant triangle. Next to it, list the various levels of leadership/hierarchy within your organization. Think about who may fall within each level, and make a list of at least one person at each level that you might be able to chat with. For example, if you are at the Manager level, you would want to identify a Vice President and Director (above you), an Analyst (below you), and other Managers (alongside you) with whom you could speak.

Now that you've identified the people you need, go talk to them! Start building buy-in from your potential champions. Share your vision, educate them on the opportunity, and invest in helping them understand how they can contribute.

Once you've done so, tick the box next to their name above! Even if your program isn't formalized yet, don't hesitate to float your ideas early.

You want to hear their thoughts. They may have recommendations on other people you should chat with or ideas that may help push your data governance program forward! Use these individuals as an informal focus group to gain valuable insights from them. You can also treat them as early customers, using Data Therapy (see page 52) to uncover their pain points and align your efforts to meet their needs.

Recruit Volunteers

"We need to get people off the sidelines and into the game"

Valerie Bonventre Calvo,
Vice President of Data Governance & Enablement (Financial Services)[26]

Volunteers are individuals who are willing to participate and collaborate with you, in addition to their existing full-time responsibilities. These individuals are curious about new initiatives and often view participation as an opportunity to learn

---

[26] https://www.linkedin.com/in/valeriebcalvo/.

and grow. They may be willing to contribute their time and energy to your data governance efforts.

Here are a few key considerations when engaging volunteers:

- Communicate the benefits of getting involved with data governance. Volunteers will have the opportunity to support high-impact organizational goals such as improving data quality to increase organizational effectiveness, expanding access to information, and shaping policies that ensure data privacy and security. Highlight opportunities for professional development, upskilling, and cross-functional networking.
- Start with low-hanging fruits: individuals who already have skill sets critical to data governance success. This

includes people in IT, data management, analytics, or finance.

- Promote volunteer opportunities through internal communication channels. Raise awareness during departmental meetings, town halls, newsletters, and one-on-one leadership conversations.

- Host informal networking events or small support groups to share insights, exchange ideas, and build connections with like-minded colleagues. One-on-one time can go a long way in sparking long-term collaboration.

Diversity, Equity, and Inclusion

When leading change, you'll need to be aware that you're working with people who have a wide range of personalities, communication styles, and lived experiences—and you may need to adapt your approach to meet them where they are. This includes diversity across cultural backgrounds, gender, age, generation, and importantly, neurodiversity.

Gartner[27] has shown that teams with cognitive diversity (that is, varied ways of thinking, habits, and perspectives) outperform homogeneous teams. Hiring a diverse team is a strong starting

[27] https://www.gartner.com/smarterwithgartner/diversity-and-inclusion-build-high-performance-teams.

point, but maintaining a diverse team requires intentional practices that foster inclusion and a sense of belonging.

To create an inclusive environment:

- Ensure your team can engage in healthy debate and share ideas without fear of judgment.
- Celebrate your team's diversity, not just demographically, but also in how they think and approach problem-solving.
- Allow for bonding opportunities (see "Party Planning" for inspiration), which foster trust, empathy, and collaboration.

Remember, inclusion is not just about who is in the room; it's about whose voice is heard, respected, and acted upon.

There may be additional considerations when working with certain areas of diversity. When working with a **neurodiverse** team, keep the following considerations in mind:

- Share the big-picture goal, but also break it down into smaller, actionable steps. Some individuals may find abstract goals overwhelming, while clear instructions can make expectations manageable and actionable.
- Don't assume someone will know what you need unless you tell them.
- Ask team members how they want to contribute and what capacity they currently have. Never assume you

know their workload or preferences—invite them to define it.

- Approach every interaction with patience and grace.
- Explain how the work connects to broader organizational goals, especially when asking people to step outside their formal roles.
- Be willing to adapt your work environment and management style. This might include rethinking how meetings are run, offering multiple ways to give feedback, or providing solo working options.
- Recognize that change can be difficult, especially for some neurodiverse individuals who may process or adapt to change differently. Offering structure and predictability can go a long way.
- Avoid interpreting a lack of eye contact as disinterest.
- Don't expect everyone to retain verbal instructions. Always follow up meetings with written task summaries that they can refer back to.

Considerations when working **cross-culturally**:[28]

- Team members may place varying emphasis on relationship-building versus task completion. Find a balance that reflects the cultural context of your team and organization.

---

[28] Further reading: *Many Cultures, One Team* by Catherine Mercer Bing (2015, Technics Publications).

- Familiarize yourself with cultural norms and etiquette to avoid unintentional misunderstandings.
- Avoid slang, idioms, or culturally specific references that may confuse or alienate others.
- Strive to maintain clear, respectful, and straightforward communication.
- Practice active listening and confirm mutual understanding by paraphrasing what you hear.

In some cultures, it may be considered impolite to disagree openly. To avoid passive agreement, create space for candid dialogue by asking open-ended questions and inviting diverse viewpoints. Always prioritize creating a safe, inclusive environment for everyone. Establish clear channels for people to report concerns when they don't feel respected or included. In data governance, people come first.

Organizational Structures for Data Governance Departments

Your data governance structure should reflect both the company's strategic priorities and the immediate goals of your program. In smaller organizations, a single dedicated resource may suffice. In larger enterprises, this model quickly becomes unsustainable. Most data governance programs begin with a core team of two to five people and expand as the organization's needs evolve. Team members are often recruited internally, as they already understand the organization's culture and operating environment. These internal relationships are especially valuable in data governance, as they require cross-functional collaboration. However, while internal hires bring context, they may lack the formal training in change leadership necessary to drive transformation, an essential component of any governance initiative.

A typical data governance team structure includes:

- A Data Governance Manager
- Data Stewards
- Data Custodians.

The IT team often acts as data custodians, supporting key data management tasks and process improvements. It is common to form data governance councils to set the strategic direction for the program. These councils typically comprise senior executives, departmental leaders, and representatives from data management. Data owners are responsible for specific data assets, while data stewards manage the day-to-day operations and maintenance of those assets. Noticeably absent from many teams are formal project management or change leadership roles. Often, these responsibilities fall to the team leader, who must manage laterally and upward to ensure alignment and accelerate implementation. For large organizations with multiple layers of hierarchy, it may be beneficial to form cross-functional teams organized by project or business domain to monitor progress and remove blockers. Executive ownership is crucial—it ensures alignment between data governance initiatives and the organization's overarching business priorities.

Data governance departments may report to different functions depending on organizational structure:

- Product/Business
- Technology/IT
- Compliance/Internal Audit.

Where the department sits should be informed by the nature of its work and your organization's culture. We see successful models across all three structures, with internal audit reporting often proving especially effective, thanks to strong alignment with governance and risk management objectives.

Some employees may find the term "governance" intimidating or bureaucratic. Don't hesitate to rename your program to better reflect its mission and tone. Alternative names to consider:

- Data Advocacy
- Data Stewardship
- Data Enablement.

When teams operate in psychologically safe and collaborative environments, individuals are more likely to act in the interest of the collective good rather than for personal gain. This cultural shift—away from self-interest and toward shared purpose—can significantly enhance the success and cohesion of your data governance team.

Take a Moment (#9)

Team building and skill building:

What kinds of skills do you think people should have?

How do you identify a good 'volunteer' for your data governance program?

What words would you use to describe these folks?

How would you find them within your organization?

Head + Heart

"Our program is not resonating with middle managers outside of governance. It's a lot of 'I don't have time for this', and 'I don't have a budget for it'. They are not fully seeing what's in it for me, they're not connecting the dots on how this is going to help them long term."

Valerie Bonventre Calvo,
Vice President of Data Governance & Enablement (Financial Services)

You must capture the hearts and minds of your team. You want people to participate not only because the data and the business reasons make sense, but also because they feel inspired. Appeal to their basic human desire to contribute to a larger purpose, feel valued, and help lead the organization toward a better future. Answer the question, "What's in it for me?" and help them connect emotionally to your mission.

In the book "The Positive Organization,"[29] Robert E. Quinn states, "If we are not committed to learning how to assume that strategic role of purpose finder and vision setter, we will remain in the tactical role of problem solver and information giver." He defines a leader by their ability to listen deeply to stakeholders and conceptualize a shared, but often unspoken, sense of purpose. He reminds us that this purpose must be:

- Put into action
- Continually clarified
- And kept top of mind for ourselves and our teams.

---

[29] Quinn, Robert E. *The Positive Organization: Breaking Free from Conventional Cultures, Constraints, and Beliefs.* Oakland, CA: Berrett-Koehler Publishers, 2015.

Logical reasons that someone may choose to be involved, "the head", include:

- Improving data management
- Making their jobs easier or more efficient
- Documenting institutional knowledge for the long term
- Meeting the goals of the organization (something they believe in, related to that)

Emotional reasons, "the heart", might include:

- A desire to be part of something bigger
- Helping move the company into the future
- Accelerating their career growth
- Networking with others outside their department
- Receiving recognition for their contributions.

Consider using this framework in presentations or one-on-one conversations. Tailor your message to appeal to both rational and emotional motivators.

In the next chapter, Hooray, we share a whole list of ideas on how to reward and celebrate your volunteers.

Take a Moment (#10)

Think about the following and write down a few ideas for things you could do:

How will you reward those who join you?

How will you make your project fun?

People might HAVE TO join you as part of their job, but list reasons they will WANT to. Change the "to do" to a "get to do".

Careers in Data Governance

Data governance professionals can come from a wide range of backgrounds and disciplines, including those with degrees in data science, data management, law, technology, or even no formal education in these fields. Who is an ideal data governance professional? Anyone with a passion for data and a sense of care for people! While there is no one-size-fits-all profile for success, this section will explore key career skills, sample job descriptions, and relevant certifications—whether you're looking to hire, advance in your role, or upskill into a governance position.

Data governance professionals often come with a combination of skills or experiences in:

- The data space (such as data analysis or management)
- Mathematics/statistics
- Technology
- The business or compliance side.

Most governance roles involve a high degree of people interaction, but the emphasis on technical, analytical, or strategic skills can vary widely depending on the organization.

Sample Job Description - Data Governance Manager

The primary role of a data governance manager is to establish and lead the data governance program. Data governance leaders may come from a variety of backgrounds. Aakriti comes from an actuarial background and has experience in non-profit organizations. We know people who have a law degree, so they come from a compliance perspective. IT executives with expertise in data management may also take over as data governance leaders. However, they all need to sharpen their skills as change leaders since they will set the direction for the department in an area new to the organization.

The job requires developing data governance policies, standards, and procedures, and collaborating with stakeholders to define data governance objectives and priorities. The leader negotiates for data governance organizational structure, budgets, and is key to hiring team members. Leaders need to have experience in data governance skills, such as knowledge of data privacy and security regulations, an understanding of data management practices, knowledge of a data governance organization structure and the specific roles each team member may play, and knowledge of setting the strategic direction for the department.

Data Governance Manager Qualifications:
- Bachelor's or Master's degrees in IT, data management, information systems, law
- Data governance certification (CDMP)
- Knowledge of industry best practices and trends
- Expert in data governance policies, standards, and procedures; keeps up with the best practices in data governance and related technology trends.

- Well-versed with data governance strategies—setting goals, prioritizing projects, and budget needs, and integrating volunteers in the data governance teams
- Good communicator, collaborator, motivator, and builds relationships with stakeholders
- Understands change management practices and techniques
- Understands data privacy and security regulations
- Has prior experience in data governance

Sample Job Description—Data Steward

Data stewards play a critical role in ensuring the company can leverage data as a strategic asset by ensuring the accuracy, integrity, and security of the organization's data assets through guiding and implementing effective data governance practices. While the scope of work can be varied, specific responsibilities may be assigned based on the size of the data governance program, the size of the team, the type of industry, and the complexity of data management. Data Stewards work with the owners of the data and with business process owners to understand the data better and ensure that business requirements are being met.

Key Responsibilities:

- Metadata Management
  - o Create, maintain, and update metadata repositories to ensure accurate documentation of data assets.

- o Collaborate with data owners on the business and technology side to enhance metadata understanding and completeness.
- Data Quality Management
- Data Lifecycle Management
- Data Classification and Sensitivity
- Data Access and Security
- Creating Data Processes
- Protecting Data Integrity
- Managing Data Lineage

Data Steward Skills:
- Database knowledge
- Communication skills
- Problem-solving skills
- Knowledge about the data management department
- Familiarity with data privacy regulations

Data Steward Qualifications:
- Bachelor's or Master's in data management or IT, or a related area
- Certification in data management or data governance (CDMP, DGSP)
- Knowledge of data governance practices
- Willingness to learn
- Experience with data governance tools and systems is a plus

Sample Job Description—Data Custodian

Data Custodians are responsible for the storage, maintenance, security, and integrity of organizational data assets. Custodians may be formally housed in the data management department and assigned to work on specific data governance projects.

Key Responsibilities:
- Data Storage and Management
- Data Access Control and Security
- Data Quality Management
- Data Backup and Recovery
- Compliance with Regulations
- Data Privacy and Confidentiality

Data Custodian Qualifications:
- Bachelor's in computer science, data management, or IT
- Understanding and experience of data management and administration concepts
- Knowledge of data privacy and security legislation
- Detail-oriented and analytical mindset
- Ability to work in a fast-paced environment
- Data governance (CDMP) and data management (DGSP) certification will be a plus

The Ideal Data Governance Professional

What makes someone ideal for a career in data governance?

There's no one-size-fits-all!

While data governance professionals can come from any background, many combine interests or experience in business, technology, mathematics, or statistics. That said, successful professionals can emerge from almost any discipline.

To explore career paths in data governance and data management, check out the Dataversity podcast My Career in Data.[30] It features interviews with professionals across the field and offers insight into how people find their way into data work.

If you or your team are looking to upskill, professional development opportunities abound in this field.

The Data Governance and Information Quality (DGIQ) Conference is one of the most influential in the space. Outside of that, conferences such as Enterprise Data World,[31] The Data Warehousing Institute (TDWI),[32] and Data Modeling Zone[33] are

---

[30] https://www.dataversity.net/podcasts/.
[31] http://enterprisedataworld.com.

[32] https://tdwi.org/.

[33] https://technicspub.com/dmz/.

also excellent for learning and networking. Dataversity regularly offers free webinars—sign up for their newsletter to stay updated.

Additionally, many cities have local chapters of professional organizations such as:

- DAMA (Data Management Association)[34]
- The Data Governance Professionals Organization (DGPO).[35]

These groups offer regional networking, training, and community support.

Remember, you don't have to have a perfect background to get started—curiosity, communication skills, and a commitment to ethical data use can take you a long way.

---

[34] https://www.dama.org/cpages/chapters.

[35] https://dgpo.org/.

CHAPTER FOUR

Hooray!

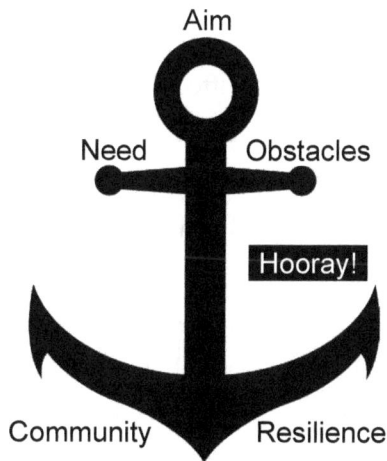

Aim

Need   Obstacles

Hooray!

Community   Resilience

Cue the Confetti, Pop the Champagne

"In data governance work, there is no return that people can feel because it's in dribs and drabs, it's hard to see the compelling picture. You're never going to feel the return if we just are focused a mile wide and an inch deep."

Valerie Bonventre Calvo,
Vice President of Data Governance & Enablement (Financial Services)

Successes create more successes!

One of the most crucial aspects of launching a new data governance program is demonstrating early successes and using them to inspire broader engagement.

The 'Hooray!' Factor will discuss how to identify your successes and communicate them effectively. When identifying successes, look both internally—within your data governance team—and externally, among volunteers, stakeholders, and other collaborators who helped make those wins possible.

In research with change management practitioners, Phillips and Klein (2023) found that communication with all organizational employees ranked twelfth of fifteen parameters, even though all sixteen change management models referred to by the researchers indicated the importance of communication.[36] However, listening to employees' and managers' concerns about the change being implemented came in the top five areas practiced by the practitioners. Providing incentives to employees to implement change was ranked last by the practitioners when thirteen of the sixteen models indicated the need for employee rewards.

It seems that there is a measurable gap in what is practiced as compared to what is recommended by the models. Perhaps that could explain the low rates of change management success as shared earlier. With that in mind, let's explore how to celebrate

---

[36] Jeffrey Phillips and James D. Klein, "Change Management: From Theory to Practice," TechTrends 67, no. 1 (2023): 189–197.

and communicate success in a way that builds momentum for your program.

Identifying Successes

You can't celebrate successes if you don't know what winning looks like! Success doesn't have to mean saving millions of dollars; small wins count too. A win for your data governance program could be securing business definitions for ten terms, finally finding the right person to assist with a specific domain, or even showing up to your meeting. It could also be as small as finding a team of volunteers to serve as your data stewards. No matter how small, these actions move your program forward and are worth celebrating.

Reframe your idea of success to encompass not only results, but also effort and progress. Even if something didn't go perfectly, the fact that someone tried or engaged is meaningful. If people are making the effort and showing up, that's a win. Recognize it. Celebrate it. Encourage more of it. Try to keep your eyes and ears open for these moments. The more you train yourself to look for success, the more you'll see it.

"We've recently instituted the concept of a weekly share. It rotates on the team, and whoever has it for the week has to reflect on something they're proud of for the week - something they think we've accomplished, whether personal or professional. It puts people on the spot to be reflective, because it may feel like every week, you don't have something to be proud of or report on. Then, at the end of the month and each quarter,

the managers create a recap to show people the work they're churning. This becomes the story we tell."

Valerie Bonventre Calvo,
Vice President of Data Governance & Enablement (Financial Services)

A note on perfection: One of the biggest mistakes you can make in data governance is chasing perfection. Perfect doesn't exist in the world of data governance—our goal is to create processes that support continuous iteration and improvement over time. When defining success, be sure to also define what "good enough" looks like. Ask: At what point have we invested enough time and resources to make meaningful progress, where adding more won't significantly improve the outcome? This isn't about lowering standards. It's about understanding that progress is incremental and meaningful change requires consistency, not perfection.

In the words of Adam Grant,[37] "Happiness lies in the range between aspirational and acceptable". Let your team operate within that range—motivated, yet never paralyzed by perfection.

As we record what our win was, we also want to capture:

- The business impact of this success (so we can share it with leadership)
- The motivation behind the win—what sparked it?
- The obstacles that were encountered along the way

---

[37] https://twitter.com/AdamMGrant/status/1767545126396502395.

Take a Moment (#11)

Visualize your ideal state - what life would be like if everything went perfectly to plan. Now, also write down what your 'good enough' looks like, what it would look like for you to be happy with how far you've come. Feel free to include potential metrics, your emotions, and the types of stakeholders that may be involved.

To keep track of your wins, you can use the following table.

Feel free to adapt the table columns to suit your organization's needs and context.

Remember: wins don't have to be big milestones. They can include actions taken, lessons learned, improved processes, new behaviors, or even small cultural shifts.

Describe the win/ success	Business Impact	Trigger/ Spark/ Motivation behind the win	What led to this success? (Secret sauce)	What barriers did you overcome and how?	Advice to help someone recreate your secret sauce	Communication of the win

The key insight here is that wins generate momentum. The most effective way to build on them is to document what made them possible, so others can replicate the success. Something worked—and that's why we celebrate it. By capturing that "something," we give ourselves a formula for future wins. The final part of the table includes a brief note on how you plan to communicate the win.

We'll dive deeper into communication strategies in the next section.

Communicate Successes Effectively!

"Collaboration and communication, for one part of my team (the data stewards), is about 80% of their work. Collaboration, communication, and documentation are critical. I joke with people. I just asked them, have you been CCD? Have you collaborated, communicated, and documented?"

David Smith, Data Governance Director (Footwear/Apparel)

Communicating well and communicating often requires a clear and intentional communication plan. In this section, we'll explore templates, practical examples, and key considerations to help you build an effective, audience-focused strategy. Remember, the goal isn't just to share updates—it's to make sure people hear them. It's not just about what we say, but also about how and where we say it. Are we using channels where people are already paying attention? Are we crafting messages in a way that's relevant and resonant to each audience?

Communication Plan Template

As part of your communications plan, figure out:

- Who do you need to/want to communicate with?
- What does this stakeholder group care about? How can you best serve their needs?
- What action would you like them to take after receiving this communication?
- What is the content of the message?
- Who is responsible for sending out this message?
- How would you like to deliver this message?
- With what frequency / when does this need to be received?
- What are your metrics or measurements of success?

Considering the questions above, the following is a communications plan template, along with sample communication ideas for each stakeholder type.

1. **Sample Communication Plan Template (DG: Data Governance)**

Stakeholder/ Stakeholder Group	Objectives/ Desired Actions	Key Message	Delivery Method	Fre-quency	Owner	Success Metrics
Executive Leaders	Sharing: Demonstrate the strategic value of DG initiatives	"Here's how DG supports our goals and mitigates risk."	Monthly email, Steering committee meeting	Monthly	DG Lead / Director	Executive acknow-ledgment, budget/ resources support

Stakeholder/ Stakeholder Group	Objectives/ Desired Actions	Key Message	Delivery Method	Fre- quency	Owner	Success Metrics
Data Stewards	Sharing/ Listening: Share updates, celebrate contributions, sustain morale	"Your work matters. Here is what we've achieved and here is what is next."	Team Meetings, Slack	Biweekly	DG Manager	Steward engage- ment, task completion, engage- ment with tools
Business Units	Listening/ Asking: Build awareness and solicit collaboration	"DG helps you work smarter, not harder."	Intranet articles, lunch and learns	Monthly / quarterly	Commu- nication Partners	Increased partici- pation or questions
All Staff	Sharing: General awareness, promote data culture/data literacy	"Why DG exists and how it supports you."	News- letter, Town Hall slide	Quarterly	Internal Commu- nications	Atten- dance, email open/click rates
Data Governance Champions (volunteers)	Sharing/ Listening/ Asking: Recognition, onboarding, motivation	"Thank you—here are the impacts you've made and what's next."	Personal emails, virtual shoutouts, cele- bratory parties	As needed	DG Coor- dinator	Retention, referrals
IT / technical teams	Asking/ Listening: Alignment of roles, update on integration efforts	"Here's how DG connects to tech initiatives and supports your work."	Project meetings, shared document ation, email blasts	Biweekly, or when a milestone is achieved	DG/IT liaison	Project milestone success

Tips for Success

- Customize the template above by department, project phase, or communication type.

- Capture next steps and action items from meetings/communications

- Add owners to ensure accountability.

- Use success metrics to track whether your messages are landing as expected/intended.

- Made adjustments as necessary.

Making Communication CLEAR

Effective communication can make or break your data governance program, so you must ensure you're doing it well and making your communication CLEAR! Valerie Bonventre Calvo, Vice President of Data Governance & Enablement and Data Governance Speaker, has created the CLEAR acronym to help us keep communication at the top of our minds and ensure it's clear and convincing. In her words, thoughtful, intentional communication moves data governance from your organization's "back office to the front page."

CLEAR[38] Communication should be:

- **Creative**. Each communication should be complementary and cohesive, with a unified look and feel that leverages multiple channels and reaches diverse audiences.

- **Lingo-free**. Avoid any language that requires data governance or even data experience to support and understand.

- **Efficient**. Data governance communications shouldn't be a chore for either the communicator or the readers. Therefore, they need to be concise and to the point, enable people to get involved, and you should be able to track progress.

- **Applicable**. You should be able to connect the dots for your audience and explain why data governance matters to them. You should also be able to tell a story instead of just giving information.

- **Regular**. Overcommunicate your message, introduce it early, and maintain a strong cadence. People often need to hear something seven times before it sinks in, so don't be afraid to repeat the same message.

---

[38] The CLEAR model was developed and is owned by Valerie Calvo, used with permission. This Dataversity Article includes a presentation by Valerie explaining the CLEAR model in more detail: https://www.dataversity.net/the-cool-kids-corner-clear-communication/.

Keeping these five factors in mind is crucial, and learning how to develop your communication skills will help your data governance program thrive.

"Something that I do in my career - whenever there is an issue, I make sure to put on my data governance hat, and run to the fire. I'll say, "Hey, I'm a data governance guy, I'm running into the fire!" If I put it out first, I'll come out, and it looks like the fire scene from movies, and here comes this data governance guy with the hat, and the fire is out because of him. At the same time, if the fire didn't go out, at least people saw that I was the only one who went in, and I came out. Very early in my career, one of my mentors told me that you always want to be the one running into the fire, but you have to let people know that you're running in, otherwise, they're going to think you're an arsonist. They'll think you started the fire."

John (Hyun Ki) Lee, Associate Director of Data Governance (Financial Services)

It's your program, you can party if you want to!

"If you can create a little bit of fun and entertainment around data governance, then at least people are curious and want to know more about it. And then open the door so you can finally step in and tell them all about why it's so important and what to do with it."

Tiankai Feng, Data & AI Strategy Director (Consulting/Professional Services)

Social gatherings are powerful tools to strengthen team cohesion and engagement. From casual coffee chats to team-building events and milestone celebrations, social gatherings can be the glue your data governance program needs to enhance team bonding. Social gatherings bring many benefits to your data governance program, such as:

- Greater engagement and morale
- A stronger desire to participate in your program

- Opportunities for relationship-building beyond work tasks.

You may notice a lack of participation from some colleagues. Perhaps they suffer from social anxiety. Plan to accommodate such colleagues as they may experience anxiety around people. Contact your HR (human resources) team, who have the necessary tools and techniques for managing such issues. Identify such people early on to help reduce their stress in social settings and share coping strategies for before, during, and after the social gathering. Research indicates that the incidence of social anxiety may be higher in large metropolitan areas than in those living in small towns. So if you are located in a metropolitan area, then be prepared to manage social anxiety to ensure the success of your social gathering plans.

Social gatherings are important for your success as they provide people with an opportunity to connect outside the work context, fostering trust, empathy, and camaraderie. Stronger relationships directly contribute to resilience, collaboration, and team success, especially during challenging periods.

In addition to these benefits, social events also allow your team to take a break from cognitively or emotionally draining work! This pause is crucial: it reduces burnout, gives the brain a reset, and helps the team recharge as a unit. As a result, people return to their work more energized, motivated, and ready to make a contribution.

Be a Party Planner (Yes, You!)

Embrace your inner party planner! Recognition and celebration don't have to be big or expensive to be meaningful. Explore creative recognition ideas from other industries, particularly for those that are both low-cost and low-effort. Keep in mind that motivation is personal and not one-size-fits-all. What excites one employee might not resonate with another, so take the time to understand your team's preferences.

Start Small

Never underestimate the power of a small gesture. Even a simple 'thank you' message or a quick shout-out in a meeting can leave a lasting impact. Gratitude builds trust.

In "Measure What Matters,"[39] John Doerr emphasizes the importance of continuous recognition as a powerful driver of engagement. John states, "As soft as it seems, saying 'thank you' is an extraordinary tool for building an engaged team. 'High recognition' companies have 31% lower voluntary turnover than companies with poor recognition cultures."

---

[39] John Doerr, Measure What Matters: How Google, Bono, and the Gates Foundation Rock the World with OKRs (New York: Portfolio, 2018).

Celebratory ideas

Idea	How to Implement It
Team appreciation event or ceremony	Host a lunch, dinner, coffee hour, or happy hour. Let the team vote on a theme or treat. Include short remarks recognizing contributions. Donuts or snacks are always well appreciated!
Build a volunteer community	Organize networking events, mentorship pairings, or small group rotations. Try cross-functional "data buddy" matches.
Themed celebrations	Celebrate Pi Day (3/14), Halloween (costume contest or pumpkin carving), Spreadsheet Day (10/17), or data trivia lunches. Include fun, team-based games.
Surprise treats or gifts	Bring desserts to meetings or mail small tokens with thank-you notes. Keep it simple and personal.
Custom awards and trophies	Give out informal awards ("Data Hero," "Governance Guru"). Use inside jokes, trophies, or certificates.
Public recognition	Use company shoutout boards, team meetings, or newsletters to highlight successes. Include quotes from beneficiaries if possible.
Spotlight stories	Feature champions or stewards in newsletters or on internal sites. Share externally if appropriate via LinkedIn or company channels.
Exclusive swag	Create custom mugs, shirts, tote bags, or stickers. Let the team vote on swag designs or slogans.
Training and certification	Sponsor professional development, such as CDMP certification. Remove barriers like fees or scheduling conflicts.
End-of-year impact report	Compile and share team wins using visuals, success stories, and estimated business value. Make it visual and easy to digest.
Rest and recharge time	Give your team an afternoon off or a no-meeting day after big wins or stressful phases.
Leadership thank you	Request thank-you notes from senior leaders. Provide templates to make it easy and authentic.
Gamify participation	Celebrate the most terms governed, best attendance, and top contributors. Include fun or surprise categories like "Quiet Hero" or "Data Comedian."

A cautionary tale: Even well-meaning recognition can fall flat if not executed thoughtfully. Imagine receiving an award that no one sees, hears about, or celebrates with you. That's not recognition—it's a missed opportunity. Recognition only works if it's seen, felt, and reinforced. Follow-through is everything!

CHAPTER FIVE

Obstacles

Facing the Friction

Leading change is hard work! It's filled with barriers—some obvious, some hidden, and they can be difficult to identify, let alone overcome. In the fifth factor of the ANCHOR model,

'Obstacles,' we'll focus on identifying what's getting in the way of progress and how to tackle it head-on. Because if we can't see what's blocking us, we can't remove it. Removing these barriers is essential—not just for current wins, but for sustaining success over time.

Although identifying barriers may not be new to you, this factor will focus specifically on the cultural and people-centered obstacles that often get overlooked but have the most impact.

Take a Moment (#12)

Think about obstacles that may be in your way to a successful data governance program. Be sure to consider all types of obstacles, including resource constraints, technological or tooling challenges, organizational barriers, communication issues, market risk or uncertainty, scope creep, planning challenges, cultural barriers, and any other potential obstacles you may encounter.

Conflict Resolution Capabilities

A significant portion of data governance work involves navigating conflicting perspectives and managing disagreements constructively. We want to hear everyone's ideas and make decisions in a way that is both inclusive and timely. Successful conflict resolution depends on open communication, active listening, mutual empathy, and a shared willingness to compromise. Your organization's culture may shape how conflict is approached, so it's essential to tailor your strategy to fit best within that context. Consider how your organization typically identifies, discusses, and resolves challenges. Look for existing, trusted mechanisms—such as structured dialogue formats or facilitation tools—that already work well within your corporate culture. Leverage those as a foundation for conflict resolution in your data governance work. Ideas to consider when resolving conflict in data governance:

- **Culture of collaboration and communication:** Are meetings taking place in person? Virtually? How do discussions take place? Typically, in organizations where open communication is encouraged, we can resolve conflicts through building consensus among team members. With a focus on resolving the conflict, you could take the lead in organizing team discussions, facilitating dialogues, or mediating as a peer.

- **Culture of adaptability":** Sometimes, competing priorities and unclear reporting relationships (such as in matrix organizations) may result in conflicts. We can propose solutions in project meetings, and if a resolution is still not found, we can escalate the issue to senior management, who may then decide on the best course of action.

- **Culture of decision making:** Who makes decisions within your organization? Are decisions made collaboratively or by senior leadership? If the emphasis is on working as a team, then team discussions may resolve conflicts. If you are a networked organization, use a consensus-building process by meeting network members.

- **Culture of creativity:** How do people find solutions to new problems? If it is through informal communication channels, collaborative discussions, and workshops, then that is what you need to follow.

- **Culture of learning:** How quickly do people learn? How do folks react to their mistakes? Do people even admit that mistakes were made or try to sweep them under the rug?

- **Culture of risk management:** Are decisions made based on risk minimization? Or are people willing to take risks if they think the solution will provide higher returns?

Please remind the audience what is at stake, creating a standardized and transparent process to ensure compliance with the law and build trust among the stakeholders.

Take a Moment (#13)

Reflect on your organization's culture regarding conflict resolution from the above lists. How can you use these existing structures to your advantage as you grow your data governance program?

Employ A Decision-Making Framework

In many organizations, decision paralysis is a common problem. We try to move things along quickly, but it seems like we can't get the right people at the table to make a decision. One of the biggest barriers to decision-making is the lack of authority or clarity of roles. The RAPID model[40] helps clarify decision accountability by listing specific roles with clearly delineated responsibilities, allowing organizations and teams to make decisions effectively yet also swiftly. We explain this model in the Appendix.

Decision-Making Bias

Sometimes, your barriers are cultural, which go deep within the organization. Organizations have memories that are sometimes carried forward unconsciously by well-meaning coworkers. When experiencing organizational bias, employees sometimes cannot recognize the systems that take power away from them and perpetuate these systems' continuation. You can end the cycle by learning to recognize organizational bias around you and helping to overcome it.

There are many types of organizational biases, but below, we'll cover a few that people tend to experience often and how to counteract them. Remember, you may not be able to change the

---

[40] Please see the Appendix for an explanation of the RAPID Model.

culture of your entire organization, but you can influence how your small team responds to information and manages change. This, in turn, will create ripple effects within your larger organizational culture.

Confirmation bias is when someone only seeks out information that will confirm what they already believe and, therefore, ignores or discredits information that doesn't support their view or ideas. When operating under this bias, people also tend to have a strong emotional reaction, either positive or negative, to information that confirms their beliefs. To overcome confirmation bias, watch out for the signs you're experiencing and how they might impact your decision-making. Encourage that all evidence is considered and valued. Seek out varying perspectives, particularly those that do not agree with your original viewpoint. Be willing to change your mind as new evidence arises.

"As humans, it's natural for us to try to attach what we already know to something new, instead of taking time to learn it. We try to implement what we have already done before in our new role or with our new team. This leads to failures as we try to recreate what we had before, trying to redo how data governance was implemented in other shops. Change the mindset by reminding people that this is completely new. Let's look at it with a fresh set of eyes. Let's take a vote. If you did good work previously, what led to success? What were the pitfalls? Take the time to think about it instead of just making fast decisions."

John (Hyun Ki) Lee, Associate Director of Data Governance (Financial Services)

Status quo bias is the idea that an action or mindset should continue simply because it has been done that way for so long. People experiencing this bias tend to be hesitant to change or "rock the boat." They prefer to maintain their current situation rather than change, whether out of fear or for other reasons. To overcome status quo bias, get down to why this fear exists. It may help to create a pros and cons list to weigh the advantages and disadvantages of changing actions or keeping things the same. Another way to counteract status quo bias is to express the current status quo as a loss. According to loss aversion theory, humans tend to assign greater weight to losses than to gains; therefore, framing the alternative option as a gain is less effective.

Sunk-cost bias is the tendency to continue with an action, mindset, or project because we've already invested a large amount of money, time, or energy in it, even if the current costs outweigh the benefits. To overcome sunk-cost bias, focus on the current and future costs and benefits, rather than past commitments. Remind your team that it is not beneficial to anyone to remain on a sinking ship. Instead of feeling wasteful or guilty about dropping an earlier commitment, focus on concrete actions. Focus your decisions on data, using key performance indicators (KPIs) to ensure that your decisions continue to benefit your goals.

Availability bias occurs when someone relies on the most easily available or remembered information, giving disproportionate weight to recent incidents and neglecting more comprehensive information. Ensure that your team reviews all relevant data, rather than just the most recent data. Ensure you're not getting stuck in a cycle of recalling only the worst information because it's the easiest to remember or talk about.

Groupthink is the tendency for a group to prioritize consensus over critical evaluation of alternatives, causing certain group members to hide their disagreement or even agree with decisions they don't agree with. This reduces creativity and can lead to suboptimal decisions, causing people in the group to feel left out or unheard. One of the biggest dangers of groupthink is that people agree with a decision while in the room, but then fail to implement it because they don't feel it's the right course of action. To overcome groupthink, ensure that everyone has a seat at the table and a voice at that table. If you feel like someone voiced an opinion and it was ignored, bring it back up in the discussion so that everyone can hear it. If a team member is being quiet, call on them specifically to speak up. If you feel the conversation is not a safe space for opposing ideas, try anonymous ways of gathering opinions.

Decision fatigue occurs when the quality of decision-making deteriorates due to the need to make numerous decisions within a short period. This can cause people to take shortcuts, resulting in suboptimal decisions. To overcome decision fatigue, encourage team members to care for their mental health. If a decision is not urgent, give people time to think about it instead of asking them to make a decision quickly. Ensure that members are taking breaks and not overexerting themselves.

Bystander apathy is a psychological phenomenon where people are less likely to assist or solve a problem when others are present, with every person in the room thinking that someone else will step in and take responsibility, resulting in no one being accountable. To overcome the bystander effect, set clear expectations of who needs to be involved and accountable for making and following through with decisions. Create a culture where, if you have the skillset to solve a problem, you must do so regardless of your position.

The Data Governance Mindset

One of the risks of working with others, particularly folks who think more in a technology mindset, is that they may make counterproductive decisions regarding data governance goals. You may experience this with your data custodians and possibly with data owners you work with. It requires a shift in mindset to perform data governance work, which sometimes goes against what we're accustomed to as data professionals or computer programmers. The following are some spaces to be cautious of.

Your technology team may be inclined to write data quality rules based on data profiling. This is incorrect. You should write data quality rules based on business requirements, not existing data. You may inadvertently write in the exact things you're trying to avoid/fix with your data and, therefore, need to write rules with a clean slate.

"You have to get data out there, let people use it, find things wrong with it, and even ask terrible questions. You must learn to love the errors inherent in the data."

Laura Madsen from her book, *Disrupting Data Governance*.[41]

---

[41] *Disrupting Data Governance: A Call to Action*, by Laura Madsen. Technics Publications, 2019.

Don't be afraid of failing, and don't be afraid of people having access to data and information before it's 100% perfect. You will never reach a point of perfection, and, therefore, this is an unachievable goal. Furthermore, the purpose of data governance is to enable people to use and analyze the data to identify issues within it.

If you're writing a data quality rule to figure out whether something is alphanumeric and also filled 95% of the time, write these rules separately. This helps with reporting and tracking issues, whereas, as a computer programmer, you may feel inclined to write these together in one line to save computing power.

You may feel inclined to have a one-to-one relationship between physical data elements (the data as it exists within your tables) and critical data elements (business metadata or the business definition of a data element). However, from a data governance standpoint, you can have multiple physical data elements related to the same critical data element. This means you can have 500 columns of data relating to only 25 critical business data elements. This may seem counterintuitive from a technological standpoint, but essential elements of data can help colleagues understand their data; therefore, we want to make our business glossaries as easy to follow and understand as possible.

Many of these issues are related to data quality specifically, so if data quality is a key focus of your data governance program, read Danette McGilvray's *Executing Data Quality Projects: Ten Steps to Quality Data and Trusted Information.*

This is not an extensive list of issues you'll face regarding the data governance mindset, so keep your eyes open for other situations where your team may need to take a step back and realign on the "right" way to complete the work. Don't be afraid to level-set and set clear expectations.

The Need for Flexibility

One of the biggest barriers to change is the lack of flexibility from the people or processes you're working with.

*In the words of **Laura Madsen** in her book Disrupting Data Governance,[42] "Rigidity in approach leads to critical failures. That's why airplane wings can flex and palm trees can withstand hurricane-force winds. Our governance structures must reflect the way we do business today; provide enough integrity to bend, but not break."*

The need for flexibility is one of the most important functions of a successful change initiative and, therefore, a successful data governance program. You can increase your team's flexibility by creating an environment that allows people to be creative, try new things, and foster a sense of trust.

---

[42] *Disrupting Data Governance: A Call to Action*, by Laura Madsen. Technics Publications, 2019.

CHAPTER SIX

Resilience

Aim

Need   Obstacles

Hooray!

Community   Resilience

The Final Anchor

The final factor of the ANCHOR model is what truly anchors your change initiative within your organization—resilience. Resilience is the capacity and ability to withstand, recover, and bounce back from adversities and setbacks faced during the change process. While change can be very fulfilling and motivating for you, your team, and the organization, change can also be challenging. Today, we may remember Dr. Martin Luther King as a changemaker, but he faced numerous challenges. Despite there being laws supporting racial equality, we still see incidents of discrimination. This is because the required adjustments to new processes take time. Some people may still be skeptical. People must be cautious and attentive when working in a new environment.

The exertion of pushing through the change may also take its toll. The implementation of change efforts may result in employee fatigue and a short-term loss of productivity as they adjust to new processes. Do build this dip in productivity immediately following change implementation in your plans. Some individuals may continue to harbor residual resistance to change and, therefore, look for signs of failure, which can result in a ripple effect of unforeseen changes, prompting business owners to adjust to new metrics to assess the effectiveness of the change. You may encounter pushback during the change process, so your ability to bounce back will determine your success. Even if you have successfully implemented a change, the perception of its effectiveness is still something you must continue to work on. Since you followed the earlier five steps (ANCHO of the ANCHOR model), you must have built a considerable amount of social capital within the organization. During this final factor of the ANCHOR model, we'll discuss the psychology of why change is difficult for individuals, how to discuss failure, and how to measure progress over time. We will stretch our crisis management muscles and discuss why we are stronger now than when we started, how we reframe negative situations to learn from them, and how we leverage this newfound strength to fuel future growth and development.

Resilience building leads to transformative behavior, innovation, and crisis management capability. Resilience strengthens your personality by fostering a positive mindset and cultivating optimism in the face of challenges. Resilience alleviates stress and builds confidence in your problem-solving abilities. Resilience leads to the development of social capital, community growth, and a robust social support network that serves as a buffer against adversity and stress. Resilience promotes flexible thinking and enhances problem-solving ability and adaptability to an ever-changing environment, strengthening your ability to find creative solutions. Resilience facilitates continuous learning and growth, encourages openness to new experiences, and promotes personal and professional development. Resilience helps hone your planning skills, incorporating contingency plans and practicing crisis management skills. You feel a sense of purpose and meaning that would motivate you for your next life phase.

Why is Change so Difficult?

Most people don't realize that change hits a core psychological trigger point in the human brain. People are not just reacting to a change in their work, but rather, a change in something that matters to them personally. Many people experience change not dissimilar to how they experience grief. This means that a person could respond similarly to a death in the family as they would to a change within the workplace. Therefore, stepping back and understanding why this change is occurring can be helpful.

The Psychology of Change

Change can be a great disruptor, not only for the organization but also for the individuals at a very personal level. We examine two key aspects of psychology that every leader should consider when initiating change. Only with an understanding of the 'grief of change' and the 'fear of change' can a leader implement measures to help people accept change. While a successful change management process may result in major organizational benefits, business unit leaders who are unconvinced and skeptical of the change may doom it to failure. On the surface, no one may acknowledge that their concerns are leading them to be skeptical. Therefore, change leaders must be cautious in how they manage the psychology of change.

The Grief of Change

People process change in much the same way they cope with grief, particularly when navigating and dealing with difficult circumstances. As a change leader, this means a few different things for you. Firstly, you have to recognize that people take time to process change. You can't tell someone about a change and immediately put it into action without expecting some backlash. Grief is an expression of love and care, which is a good thing; we want to encourage our employees to care about their work. However, the consequence is that, like grief, everyone will process the change at their own pace. Also, you'll likely see strong displeasure before someone can accept change. It's essential to maintain their attention and help shift this negativity into a neutral state.

If you compare the different factors of grief presented by Dr. Elizabeth Kübler-Ross in her 1969 book, they are very similar to the stages people go through in the change management process. As a result, her foundation adapted her grief management model to one that caters to change.[43] According to the Kübler-Ross Change Curve®, people go through change in the following five stages:

Stage 1: Shock and Denial
Stage 2: Frustration or Anger
Stage 3: Depression
Stage 4: Experiment
Stage 5: Decision and Integration

Surprised? Does that sound like something very personal to you?

The usual reaction to suggested change is one of shock. Shock is short-lived, as it may be due to people not having enough

---

[43] https://www.ekrfoundation.org/5-stages-of-grief/change-curve/.

information or the fear of the unknown. People deny the change as they are comfortable with the status quo, feel threatened, or may experience a fear of failure.

The next stage is that of frustration or anger. People may feel suspicious or skeptical of the change. They may try to paint the organization, department, or individual as the perpetrator of the problem. They try to focus on others as the reason for their anxieties.

Once their anger wears off, the typical reaction is one of feeling depressed. People may experience low morale at this stage as they may feel isolated. They may accept that the change has taken place. And yet, they may experience self-doubt and anxiety.

As they accept the inevitability of change, a more enthusiastic mood emerges. They may reconcile with the certainty of change, start working with it, and experiment with the new systems. They begin their upward trajectory of experiencing positive feelings as they realize that change offers them new opportunities.

The final factor is learning to work with the change and accepting it as the new way of life. People become reinvigorated, and their productivity and energy levels start to increase.

Moving along these factors is not particularly linear; people will bounce back and forth between factors, and you might feel like they're taking one step forward and two steps back. Continue to express care and keep them engaged.

Fear of Change

For many people, change may be synonymous with fear. Fear is an emotional reaction experienced until we examine the information behind the change and start thinking about it consciously. If examined consciously, fear can result in knowledge and understanding. The two main causes of fear are:

- **Loss of connection**: The fear of not being wanted, respected, or valued by anyone else. People fear the unknown and dread the possibility of potential risks. The new environment is not familiar and thus may pose a threat to their safety and security. Change may disrupt established routines, relationships, and structure.

- **Loss of autonomy**. The fear of being restricted, overwhelmed, imprisoned, or otherwise controlled by circumstances beyond our control. People need to confront their limitations and vulnerabilities. Making the data available to the organization may result in losing control. Others may find faults with what was done. Can that lead to more questions than answers?

In the book "Transitions,"[44] William Bridges and Susan Bridges highlight that a person's reaction to change within the workplace differs based on what is going on in their personal life. If you're going through a significant transition in your personal life, even a minor change in your professional life can lead to a high degree of

---

[44] William Bridges and Susan Bridges, *Transitions: Making Sense of Life's Changes*, 40th Anniversary Edition (New York: Balance, December 17, 2019), ISBN 0738285404.

imbalance. It's also important to remember that every change begins with an ending. "We have to let go of the old thing before we pick up a new one, not just outwardly but inwardly, where we keep our connections to people and places that act as definitions of who we are." - William Bridges, "Transitions." When we reframe our idea of change as a two-part process, the first being a loss that someone is incurring and the second being a new process that they're gaining, we might be able to better put ourselves in the shoes of the people we're trying to change. We must help guide the emotions of our teams and help them come to terms with both the positive and negative aspects of change. Here are some tactics that you can use to overcome the fear:

- Acknowledge the feeling
- Bring in logic
- Plan for the fear
- Talk about it—name it
- Give them connection and autonomy through the process.

In short, involve them right from the beginning. Make them feel that this is their project. Listen to their ideas and give them credit for them. Fight fear with the fear of missing out, of losing an opportunity to grow and learn. Plan social networking events that bring people from across the organization together. Take an opportunity in team meetings to acknowledge their contributions. Nothing can beat the logic of change, which benefits the organization. Hammer in the benefits to bring them back to consciousness and away from an emotional reaction. Don't hide the consequences of change. Think about how to position the change positively.

New processes and systems may take time to understand. Perhaps the process being replaced was a temporary way around the old processes, but this one is a more permanent and thought-through process. Perhaps the new process is required to keep up with the changed environment and maintain a competitive advantage.

The possible loss of control over some data is in the wider interests of the organization. In the old school of thought, data may be power. However, in the new scheme of things, sharing data may help with better decisions. The possibility of others finding faults with how things were done in the past. Make sure that people are recognized for the good work they did earlier. The changed process is not a reflection on a job done poorly, but an acknowledgment that this process is important for the company and thus there is a greater focus of the organization on this process.

Once people start accepting the change, they will acknowledge its benefits and become supporters of the change. Leadership is about managing people's fears during this period of transition.

Hard Lessons Learned

It is well known that we should learn from our mistakes and use failures to drive future successes forward. However, does that mean we no longer fear making a mistake? Most of us react with our emotions, but may fail to consider failure a step to success. So, reflect on what didn't go well to avoid it next time. Failures help build organizational resilience by building a repository of knowledge for others to learn from. Remember, resilience building is not about never falling; it's about how quickly you get up after your fall. There is always a risk of failure when you try something new. You are taking risks when trying to restructure how data assets are stored, accessed, and used within your organization. Here is an activity for you to learn from your falls.

Types of Capital Developed During the Change Process

In economics, 'capital' refers to assets or resources used to generate wealth. During the change process, you are helping develop several 'capitals'. These are Institutional, Political, Human, and Economic capital. Most of the time, when we estimate the value contribution of a project, we only assess the economic savings or revenues that the project might help us save or earn. However, the intangible capital, such as building institutional capacity, capability, and knowledge accrued through this project, is equally important, as are the social networks, connections, or relationships that you make. Many of your team members may acquire new skills that enhance their value to the organization. Let's discuss these capitals next.

Take a Moment (#14)

List failures your data governance program has experienced and what you have learned from them. What are the areas of improvement? How can you avoid these failures in the future?

Institutional Capital

As the name suggests, it is the resources, capabilities, and relationships that the institution possesses. Besides financial, brand, and intellectual property resources, institutional capital means their capacity for:

- Developing a solution to a new problem
- Taking quick action when faced with unanticipated issues
- Speed of the decision-making process
- The degree of information that the organization possesses
- How flexible they are in responding to changes
- How strong and complementary their relationships are with their suppliers, vendors, and industry networks

Essentially, the organization's knowledge and expertise set them apart from their peers and competitors. These unique qualities may lead to higher revenues and greater market success than their competitors. Data governance and change management processes enhance the organization's capability to find compliant solutions, collaborate across departments, and make tough decisions about data nomenclature, access, and control.

Influence

This bank of goodwill and "chits" enables you to access crucial information, secure professional favors, and expedite processes. Being in the good books of multiple people in your organization may help you with collaboration, partnerships, and being given advance alerts on possible issues. Influence, also known as political capital, is the intersection of three crucial assets:

- **Social Capital:** Close relationships with key people and looser (but still positive) connections to many acquaintances. In essence, social capital refers to who you know. Being recognized and valued among industry peers and across social networks can help individuals gain insight into the future of their industry.
- **Intellectual Capital:** Your degrees, experiences, credentials, and the skills that you bring to your job, as well as those that probably got you the job. Intellectual capital comprises what you know.
- **Psychological Capital:** Encompasses how you relate to others, including traits such as curiosity, empathy, emotional intelligence, learning ability, integrity, and coachability. These are often described as "soft skills," though since they are highly sought-after qualities, we prefer to call them "power skills."

Influence is one of the most important assets for an individual as an employee and is crucial for the organization. The greater the level of influence in the organization, the more interconnected its employees are and work in close coordination. Higher influence may lead to less bureaucracy and greater efficiency within the organization. Change management projects require the data governance teams to collaborate with business owners, understand their needs, and develop partnership solutions. They need to build relationships with business leaders and their peers in those departments, as well as the IT and data management departments.

Human Capital

Human capital refers to the attributes people possess, such as knowledge, skills, and experience. Your proficiency and expertise increase with practice over time. Your team learns new skills and hones their existing skills. That means the economic value of a worker increases with their experience and skills. We can advance human capital through education and training. Human capital may comprise the intelligence and skills of an organization's workers, as well as their health, loyalty, and punctuality. We can nurture human capital through motivation, recognition, and engagement. As such, it is an intangible asset or quality that isn't (and can't be) listed on a company's balance sheet. By managing, nurturing, and investing in human capital, organizations can unlock opportunities for growth and success. Data governance is a rapidly evolving field. Therefore, executing projects in the data governance field enhances the competency and capability of people involved in the projects. These include people responsible for data governance, business departments, IT, and data management. Senior managers may need to decide who has access to what data. Therefore, data governance projects engender collaboration and cooperation among senior leadership. High-quality data that is uniquely positioned to support an organization is difficult, if not impossible, to reproduce and provides a competitive advantage to the organization. People with skills and experience in data governance, similarly, can create a competitive advantage that is difficult for others to replicate.

Economic Capital

Economic capital is a measure of risk expressed in terms of financial resources. These are funds allocated to cover any unexpected losses, ensuring the organization remains solvent and stable. Organizations face a variety of risks, including credit risk, market risk, operational risk, and liquidity risk. Financial experts in the organization develop models to assess an organization's risk and the amount of capital required to cover it. By implementing proper data governance processes, the organization reduces its risk of data security and privacy breaches, thereby decreasing the need for financial capital.

KPIs of Your Change Management Program

"If you work in data, you don't get recognized until something goes wrong and you fix it. If something breaks, everyone goes on high alert. I can't do this. I can't do that. Then, when I go and fix it, they'll say, oh, thanks, John, for fixing this in five hours! If something bad happens and it's fixed, we're celebrated, but if the data is good, no one bats an eyelid because that's the expectation. When something bad happens and we fix it, I'm on the rooftops shouting it out! It's hard to get people to recognize the value of it without somebody like me to scream it out. So, from an overall enterprise organizational perspective, I made sure that our key performance indicators have connections with the cleanliness of data because it's been good and there are no issues. It should be part of our performance at the end of the year."

John (Hyun Ki) Lee, Associate Director of Data Governance (Financial Services)

Take a Moment (#15)

Think of the last project you were involved in. Can you recall one example of Institutional, Influence, Human, and Economic capital that resulted from this project? Give yourself a "pat on the back" if you can list two examples for each kind of capital.

Your change management program needs to be measured so that you can continue to institutionalize the knowledge of how these programs work. Resources need to be invested in documenting the program at every stage so that future programs can be more efficient and of higher quality. Every program may be different and have its own nuances. Therefore, time to completion cannot be the only measure of success. You may assess the change management program's effectiveness by breaking it down into two high-level stages.

- Phase 1: Project planning and implementation
- Phase 2: Post-implementation, steady rate

Phase 1: Project Planning and Implementation Phase

The goal is to monitor the change management program's progress, performance, and success in relation to its objectives and targets. This can help the program leader assess the project's health, make informed decisions to ensure its success, and identify areas for improvement. Some of these project measures are hard (e.g., project timeline), while others are soft (e.g., stakeholder satisfaction). Hard measures will have specific numbers, such as start and end dates for project implementation. Soft measures may be based on feedback, such as the level of stakeholder satisfaction with the project. Consider the list of key performance indicators (KPIs) for the project itself and select what works best for you:

- Monitor the project timeline against the plan

- Monitor budget spending against the plan
- Any increase in scope during the project or scope creep over the original scope
- Resource utilization against plan, including people, equipment, materials, and budget
- Risk management against the plan, whether the risk response plans and risk mitigation strategies were sufficient to manage the risks experienced
- Stakeholder satisfaction, gather feedback from those involved
- Quality achieved versus expectations, perform a project audit to determine if proper procedures were followed and whether corners were cut
- Communication plan effectiveness, project progress updates, and revisions to the project.

Phase 2: Post-implementation, steady rate phase

- **Benefits Realization:** Track cost savings, productivity improvement, and business unit satisfaction.
- **User Issues Resolved:** Track adoption and engagement by measuring what issues users have and how many of them have been resolved. For example, compliance rates have improved, and fewer data privacy issues are being faced. You may track the status of each issue, such as identified, in progress, resolved, closed, etc. You may find that some issues were no longer relevant as you

progressed with the project. You could also track the time to resolution.

- **Risk Reduction:** Check whether the risk of compliance failure and data loss has reduced.
- **Knowledge Enhancement:** Check if the project planning process and implementation have been properly documented, and assess how much time and effort may have been saved for future projects as a result of the documentation.
- **Quality of Results:** Measure whether the project delivered quality results over a specified period (e.g., 6 months, 1 year, etc.).
- **Stakeholder Feedback:** Track how satisfied various stakeholders are with the project deliverables.

We need to document the pre-, during, and post-project status. That can help assess the progress made by the change program. Also, it becomes institutional capital as future projects may benefit from this knowledge.

Maturity Model

A data governance maturity model helps you assess your program's progress and identify areas for improvement. Multiple maturity models can be used to measure your program, and we recommend completing this assessment at least once or twice a year to facilitate comparison.

Take a Moment (#16)

Think of the last project that you completed. Share KPIs that were used. Additionally, consider other KPIs to measure. Were the project steps, plans, and outcomes documented? Share your assessment of the quality and contribution made by the project. Do you think the other stakeholders would agree with you? If not, what were the differences, and how can they be resolved?

The DAMA Netherlands chapter has a working group where volunteers have created a very robust Maturity Model, which is free to download and use from their website,[45] and is our preferred model. However, there are numerous maturity models available online that could also be considered.[46] The book "Data Strategies for Data Governance" by Marilu Lopez also dives deeply into maturity models.[47]

---

[45] DAMA Netherlands Working Group page (you will need Google Translate to put this in English): https://dama-nl.org/werkgroepen/werkgroep-data-maturity/, with the most recent model at time of publishing: https://dama-nl.org/wp-content/uploads/2025/02/DAMA-Maturity-Scan-V2.0-_English.xlsx.

[46] This article talks about numerous models that might be used: https://www.dataversity.net/data-governance-maturity-assessment-model/.

[47] *Data Strategies for Data Governance*, by Marilu Lopez (2023, Technics Publications).

CHAPTER SEVEN

Reflection

Looking Back to Lead Forward

The ANCHOR model evolved as we encountered new challenges and incorporated our experiences to help structure and implement change. We hope you can use it to influence change within your organizations as well.

Now that we've discussed our six factors of change, how will you apply this to your organization? Use the next few pages to develop an action plan for implementing your ANCHOR model. For starters, you may have completed the 'Take A Moment' self-reflection exercises in this book. If not, consider completing them. Remember, you need not be perfect. 'Take Moment' exercises could be used as your starting points for each factor of the ANCHOR model. Here is a reminder of the six factors:

Apply/Use the ANCHOR Model

- **Factor 1, Aim:** Find clarity around the scope of your data governance program, gather opportunities, and prioritize your work based on the resources at your disposal.

- **Factor 2, Need:** Align your goals with your organization's goals and communicate business value to your leadership.

- **Factor 3, Community:** Find 'volunteers' across your organization that can help you achieve your goals; engage their heads and hearts; eventually hire a team of your own.

- **Factor 4, Hooray!** Celebrate your volunteers and team members by identifying and communicating successes and making people feel appreciated.

- **Factor 5, Obstacles:** Identify barriers that are in your way, particularly organizational and cultural barriers, and work to remove them.

- **Factor 6, Resilience:** Understand what causes change initiatives to fail, and use your understanding of the ANCHOR process to overcome those issues; measure growth and build on your momentum, and ensure the change initiative takes root.

Share your feedback on the book and its contents with us. Situations change, and we would love to hear from you to help us fine-tune this book. So, do write to us with your views.[48]

---

48 Please reach us via AnchorYourChange.com.

Take a Moment (#17)

What can you put into immediate action for each factor of the model? Indicate those you can address immediately and start working.

A:

N:

C:

H:

O:

R:

We would love to hear about your experiences. Are they similar to those presented in this book? Did the ideas in this book help resolve some of the questions you had in mind? Capture them in this next activity.

Take a Moment (#18)

What are your biggest takeaways from this book?

1.

2.

3.

4.

5.

What are some areas that you still have questions about or need to do more research on?

1.

2.

3.

4.

5.

Charting the Course on Your Change Management Journey

We enjoyed sharing nuggets of our experience driving change, especially in the context of data governance. Data has always been there, but its context has changed. Arvind remembers when he could get all his customers' data on a floppy drive, each holding 1.44 MB of data. Now, we are talking zettabytes—21 zeroes or a trillion gigabytes. That is not just because of an immense number of customers, but also because the amount of information we store per customer has increased tremendously. Every click a customer makes on a company's website is tracked. As we write this book using Google Docs, Google tracks our searches and activities. We are sure their AI is trying to determine what we are doing and what content they should serve us next.

AI is the next big thing poised to impact this industry. AI may be able to find data quality issues such as duplicates, inconsistencies, and inaccuracies. Natural language processing algorithms could analyze text data into categories and entities. Machine learning and pattern recognition may take over the task of identifying and protecting personal data, as well as ensuring privacy. AI-driven automation tools may manage policy enforcement. AI algorithms may identify data flows and relationships to identify data lineage. AI-powered analytics tools may be used to generate reports for compliance and management of data governance tasks. Predictive analytics can help identify risks associated with compliance and data issues.

What role does change leadership play in the era of AI? Will the ANCHOR model be useful in the context of AI?

We believe that the human brain lies at the heart of all automation and artificial intelligence. People must apply these tools, train them for the tasks at hand, and update them as needed based on changing environments and contexts. Data strategies will continue to be driven by people and their leaders, who will drive data governance. The ANCHOR model can manage people's expectations, motivate them, and make them feel their voices are heard and valued. So, our prognosis is that change leadership will continue to play an even bigger role in the era of AI. A model like ANCHOR may be even more impactful as humans stop handling routine, mundane tasks, such as finding duplicates or errors in the data, and focus on more cerebral, strategic thinking. AI will allow better use of employees' knowledge and expertise. Effective change leadership is a crucial skill that will significantly impact the success of a data governance program.

Thank you for joining us as you read the book and reflect on its content. We wish you all the best on your change leadership journey!

CHAPTER EIGHT

Case Study

This is Arvind. I share an application of the ANCHOR Change Leadership model in the context of a new product launch. Let us assume that we are launching a new credit card called the 'Extra Credit Line Card.' The details that follow are based on my experience launching credit cards.[49] We already researched the need for this credit card amongst consumers and identified the target audience for it. We also defined the features for this credit card based on our research. We leveraged the existing infrastructure—call center, card processing center, and our existing card system—to host the new credit card. We had to make sure that the staff bought into the need for this new product, as well as the need to set up the new processes required to support

---

[49] For full disclosure that while this example is based on actual experience with credit card launches, the ANCHOR Change Leadership model was not available to me at that time. Therefore, the details here are based on categorizing the various activities into the six model factors. To ensure anonymity of the company for whom I launched the credit card, the contours of the launch have been changed.

the launch. Quality customer support is crucial to building trust for this card. We needed to identify goals that align with corporate priorities, senior manager goals, and the resources of our peers across various departments, so that they can support the credit card launch with appropriate systems, processes, and resources. Let us go through each of the six factors of the ANCHOR change leadership model to see how these factors could have helped with the launch.

Factor 1. Aim

Since we were spearheading the credit card launch, we first needed to set our goals. In terms of features, we identified that the new credit card must offer a 20% higher credit limit than our current credit card. That was an open opportunity that our consumer research had unearthed. Since we offered classic, gold, and platinum credit cards, the additional credit lines were also available across the three card versions. Each version offered 20% higher credit than was currently offered. We could either start with goals, such as determining how many cards to obtain and what the revenue would be, or arrive at those numbers in consultation with other departments using 'data therapy.' However, we needed some goals as a starting point so that the other departments could estimate the resources needed to support us for this launch. So we aimed for some initial numbers, such as: (a) targeting around 100,000 customers in the first year, and then adding another 75,000 customers every year, resulting in a total of

400,000 card members over the next five years. (b) From experience, we knew that approximately 5% of card members cancel their accounts each year, and around 1% become delinquent. So, the net cards at the end of five years will be around 350,000. (c) Since this card offered extra credit, we expected those who revolve their credit card payments to be attracted to this extra benefit at no additional cost. Therefore, we expected to earn a 5% higher average revenue than our existing cards. Therefore, we had two key goals: to sign up 350,000 net cards over five years and to earn 5% higher revenue than our existing card. (d) Assuming the standard marketing and advertising costs, we should be able to earn 2% higher profits than our existing cards, given the higher interest rate earned on the credit balances.

Armed with these numbers, market research findings, target audience definition, and a broad advertising/communication plan, we engaged in 'data therapy' sessions with the card application processing, card issuing, and customer service departments that cover the call center, card debt collection department, and the finance department. The data therapy sessions focused on understanding their needs, alert them of our goals, understand their current processes and what changes might be required to support the new card product, whether they have sufficient resources to support the new card launch, what kind of training their people/others might need, what new processes they may need to set up, was there any information they needed to collect on the card application so that they could assess eligibility for the extra credit limit, and whether the assumptions for our numbers are adequate, and so on. Going with some initial numbers helped start the conversation more objectively. I took notes during this session so that I could summarize the discussion and confirm what action items emerged. Please note that the data therapy sessions are confidential, and therefore, no individual names need to be mentioned in the discussion summary document. Since we had presented our data and goals, we listened to the other departments without trying to find a solution on the spot. During the session, we made sure that we presented the need to add the new card and how it aligns with the organizational mission and vision.

Factor 2: Need

Now that we have collected the issues, concerns, and ideas from various departments, we have strengthened our launch plan by incorporating them as appropriate. I did share a summary of our discussions and our decisions with the departments/people with whom I interacted for data therapy. Unlike a data governance function, which is a support function, the marketing department has its goals and targets on which they are assessed. So the issues, concerns, and ideas from other departments needed to be weighed against our goals. There can always be conflicting concerns. For example, a higher credit limit means greater risk of delinquency. How do we mitigate that so that our portfolio remains profitable? The risk department had to come up with suggestions for that. That also means that the risk department targets for the extent of delinquency need to be raised upwards. For that, the senior management had to buy into the whole program. Such negotiations with the risk department and the senior managers may result in a revision of our launch goals. Therefore, the goal setting was an interdependent and iterative process.

Next, we developed a business case that calculated the estimated value the new credit cards may bring to the organization, which includes:

- Financial value
- Qualitative value
- Risks due to the launch.

We presented the business case to our senior managers, who shared their views given the importance of the consumer need that we had uncovered. We presented a budget to launch the card. In this case, once the country management approved the business case, it had to be presented and approved by senior managers at the Asia Pacific level and the product heads at the corporate headquarters. Once there was a go-ahead, then my senior managers opened the doors for us across various departments. So it was of utmost importance that our senior managers bought into the business case for our launch. Just for your information, the whole exercise from researching the needs to building the business case, and then getting approvals for the card launch, took us around two years of intense collaboration across departments.

Factor 3: Community

The success of a new product depends on the people who support the various services that define the product. In our case, these services include new card application processing, customer support, billing, credit line management, and loyalty program management. If we had continued to follow the existing rules for approving new card applications, we might have rejected good applications. If customer calls are not appropriately answered, then customer satisfaction may be at risk. If customers did not experience the higher credit limits, then they may not see value in our credit cards. Therefore, it is crucial to go through the entire life cycle of a new customer with our company carefully.

With a new card program in place, it is crucial to gather feedback on customer experiences and their impressions of the new product. For example, what kinds of questions are customers asking? How are the delinquency rates for the new card program tracking, and what measures are being taken to recover outstanding balances? Therefore, it is crucial to communicate the new card program to the rest of the company. This can only happen if the managers and team members in other departments of the company consider this new card program as their own. They need to feel that they are a part of this new product launch and so feel a sense of ownership. Thus, we need to get them involved with the new program—what could work well, and what could lead to failure. How can customer segments be targeted and recognized as part of a special card program? The employees of the company are the best advocates for the new card program, and they could put in a good word with their acquaintances about the card.

So, we started mapping all the departments and identifying all the relevant people whom we need to get on our side. We especially targeted employees who would be involved with the new cardmembers. We began a conversation with each of them and took note of their thoughts. We needed to build a community around the launch of the new credit card. At that time, there was no internet or social media. Therefore, we needed to have in-person or over-the-phone meetings. Today, we can establish a knowledge-sharing group where we post updates about the new card program, including our progress on the launch, the design of the new card, and the status of the card applications.

We did make provisions for rewards and recognition. Thank you notes, gifts recognizing helpful feedback, and socializing over lunch or coffee were a few simple acts that made everyone feel valued. We invited the whole company to a card launch party where, through a number of games, the features and the value of the new card program were highlighted. The senior management team had put together a task force for the launch of the card. The task force members represented different levels from different departments. Hierarchy issues may arise in the task force. Therefore, the community we created became even more critical to ensure a cohesive and supportive working environment.

Factor 4: Hooray!

Celebrating wins is a much underestimated step in change management. It is the easiest act that can bring your community together. Creating an occasion and sharing treats in the office that everyone can enjoy together is a simple way to bond. Follow the protocol that already exists in your office—bring a box of donuts, or take the team out for lunch. Give away rewards, tokens of appreciation, or go out of your way to express gratitude. Recognize contributions in town hall meetings. Include recognition letters that go into their personal files. Ensure that all key individuals essential to your mission are included.

Factor 5: Obstacles

Now that we have made new friends in the office, we can expect feedback and suggestions on the launch plans on a regular basis from them. We captured all these ideas and incorporated as many of them as we thought would enhance the card launch success. Sometimes, the most innocuous feedback may make all the difference. During one of my card launches, a colleague recommended that we take extra care in training the call center staff on the protocols for this new card. We did that and realized how poorly trained the call center staff were in handling typical customer calls. That training saved us many card members as we helped create the call scripts. We had to rewrite letters sent to card applicants who were rejected to make the tone more positive. Even though they may not have qualified for this credit card, they were encouraged to apply for other credit cards in our portfolio. The other credit cards may not have as stringent a criterion to qualify as this credit card, which came with an extra credit limit.

We presented information and updates to the task force, which provided official guidance on the necessary actions. Many areas were new to them. Some of them may not understand the areas besides their own. We were experimenting with new marketing techniques, and therefore, we did a test run. For example, the new credit card could be cross-sold to current card members. For that, we needed to establish a criterion to pre-approve current card members for the risk team to review. People carry multiple cards and switch between them. If we don't sell them our credit card, someone else will. Therefore, it is better to make an offer without hesitation. This may not go down well with other departments that may have concerns about cannibalization of the existing card business. So, we may need to identify such card members first. For example, they may not be very profitable for the company, but they may be excited by the higher credit limit available on the new credit card. Low profitability may indicate that these customers may be preferring other credit cards over ours. This is just one example, but establishing relationships with the risk department and the IT person responsible for the cardmember database was crucial for completing this task.

A new card launch comes with many new ideas and related obstacles. We may not be able to resolve or find an amicable resolution to all of them. So, we assign a timeline for each activity and priority levels to each of them. If we believe it is crucial for the success of the new card launch, then we will assign more time to it.

Factor 6: Resilience

This is such an important step, but it is often ignored. Resilience is about building on and maintaining the momentum created in times of necessity. We maintained the friendships built during the card launch process and carried forward the goodwill that we had generated. We continued sharing the card launch numbers with the core group that is part of our community. We cataloged the new learnings gained during the launch and shared them as a follow-up to the launch. We enhanced the skills of some employees through training or special tasks, such as identifying existing card members who could be sold the new credit card. We built on such knowledge to identify those who could be cross-sold other credit cards. We implemented some card activation or loyalty enhancement programs that were modified based on card member feedback. We used that learning to review the loyalty programs for other card programs. We revisited ideas not achieved during the launch to see if there was merit in pursuing them for the next credit card launch or for other cards in our portfolio.

In essence, we applied the ideas that worked for this one launch to further enhance the value of the company. Small steps, such as building resilience, not only added to our skill sets and strengthened our profile, but also made us thought leaders who built a lifelong friend circle. I continue to be in touch with many of my colleagues with whom I worked on the credit card launch that I just talked about. I went on to launch other credit cards for other companies, and the learning carried on. Therefore, pursuing a structured program, such as the one using the ANCHOR change leadership model, can help not just build organizational memory but also your career.

Afterword

One of the privileges of being a pioneer in a field is seeing others build on your work in a way that advances what is possible, what is practical, and what success looks like. Aakriti and Arvind have done that for Data Governance, and I'm so glad.

With their model, we have a new way of following up on a claim we early adopters have been making for over twenty years: "Successful Data Governance is over eighty percent communication."

We said this because we held a fundamental belief: *Working with data is different from working with people.* That is:

- Data and technology are <u>complicated</u>. They exist in systems that have many moving parts. These systems exist in a constant state of change. Their managers must focus on meeting ever-changing needs: fixing problems, accommodating new requirements, adopting new and improved components and models. They must know how to break complicated problems into smaller ones that can be solved.

- Human beings are <u>complex</u>. People are beyond complicated, and they operate within <u>complex</u> organizational systems. Those who influence them must know how to simultaneously address multiple facets and features of complex people and organizations.

In those early days, we predicted that the lines between Data Management and the new Data Governance discipline would become more distinct. Data Management disciplines would evolve significantly to accommodate increasingly complicated technical systems. Data Governance, on the other hand, would focus on policy, decision rights within the organization, and working with humans, in all their complexity.

Here's what else we taught: Change is constant.

This was important to know, we said, because in any organization that needs formal Data Governance, staff are proactively and reactively responding to changes in technical environments and organizational needs. Data Governance professionals would need to guide that change, convincing others of the best ways to respond to it.

One thing wouldn't change, we said: A core competency of this new Data Governance discipline would always be *communications*. Leaders and practitioners would always need to describe how to govern data and its systems and convince stakeholders to do their part. In our teaching, we adapted lessons from Marketing, Public Relations, and Technical Communications. We focused on how one individual could learn to understand and influence other individuals.

We weren't wrong. But "marketing" Data Governance wasn't a great fit for all organizational environments.

Which brings us to now. Have you ever had a moment where you slap your forehead and say "Of course!" That's how I reacted when I first heard Aakriti speak about their approach. She described the human side of Data Governance through the lens and learning of Organizational Change Management. And these learnings – which had historically been taught using HR-related jargon and case studies – were presented as skills to be applied to the human side of governing and managing constantly changing data environments.

My head slap helped me reframe what we were often communicating about. Change! Of course.

The ANCHOR model makes a lot of sense. It acknowledges communications skills, while putting them into the context of Organizational Change Management. This book (and the authors' classes) present scenarios where Data Governance staff need to communicate with others about:

- Changes regarding data (The data itself, models, architectures, systems, tools)

- Changes to rules (Policies, compliance requirements, data quality rules, access and sharing, privacy)

- Changes to documentation (Procedures, definitions, catalogs, control objectives)

- Changes to processes (Decision-making, risk management, development lifecycles)

- Changes to roles and responsibilities
  (Stewardship, governance, management)

The ANCHOR model addresses more than communication, of course. It provides a mnemonic and model that can be applied to any program that relies upon strong, consistent organizational change management. And it teaches the model in an accessible manner.

As you work your way through the model, take a moment to pause with me on the fourth facet (the H in ANCHOR): **H**ooray!

Celebrate what you're learning and doing. And know that you're continuing a strong tradition, while taking it into the future. As you make your way past **O**bstacles and acquire **R**esilience, take another moment to ensure you've memorized the ANCHOR mnemonic so you can explain it to others.

After all, as you participate in Data Governance, addressing what is possible, practical, and has been proven to be successful, you're going to spend a large percentage of your time communicating. And there's nothing like a good model and mnemonic to help you along.

Gwen Thomas
Founder, The Data Governance Institute

Author Bios

Dr. Arvind Agrawal, MBA, Ph.D.

Dr. Arvind Agrawal spent over 30 years of his career as a marketing professional, working hands-on with a variety of consumers within the financial services industry in India and the Asia-Pacific region. He has led multi-million-dollar marketing budgets for multiple Fortune 500 companies, including American Express, GE Capital, and VISA International, as well as for smaller companies such as Contract Direct, Fair Isaac, and NIIT. Through these experiences, he has successfully introduced multiple financial products by focusing not just on the launch itself, but also on the culture and process changes required within the company.

After a successful professional career, Arvind chose to relive his college days and return to pursue a Ph.D. in Consumer Behavior, researching the factors that influence decision-making. He is now an Assistant Professor of marketing at the University of Nebraska-Omaha, where he shares knowledge with undergraduate and master's students. Arvind's first book, *"How India Found Its Feet"*, shares the economic growth of India during the 1990s and early 2000s, through a collection of interviews with the people who led the change in the economic makeup of the country, distilling the essence of their successes. Arvind frequently publishes articles on topics such as marketing, entrepreneurship, the financial industry, and consumer psychology.

Feel free to connect with Arvind on LinkedIn via https://www.linkedin.com/in/arvind-agrawal/.

Aakriti Agrawal, MBA, CDMP

Aakriti Agrawal, MBA, CDMP Practitioner, is a Senior Manager of Data Governance at American Express, a Fortune 100 company. She has a Master's degree with a focus in organizational and nonprofit change from the University of Nebraska-Lincoln and has spent the entirety of her career in data management and data governance. On the side, she enjoys philanthropy work—she is a serial nonprofit founder.

She co-founded her first nonprofit, Girls Code Lincoln, which teaches middle school girls to computer program in Lincoln, Nebraska, as she was herself learning to code. Her second nonprofit, the Nonprofiting Org, provides entrepreneurial support to nonprofit founders. Through her professional and philanthropic experiences, Aakriti has demonstrated effective change leadership by generating buy-in, developing processes, and creating robust programs that grow and thrive.

She has been recognized with the Inspire Founders Award and the Emerging Young Leaders Award, has been nominated to the Forbes 30 Under 30 List, has given a TEDx talk, and serves on numerous boards of national and international nonprofits. Aakriti is a frequent speaker on topics such as data governance, change management, female representation in STEM, and entrepreneurship.

Feel free to connect with Aakriti on LinkedIn via https://www.linkedin.com/in/aakritiagrawal/.

Disclaimer: This book is an amalgamation of thoughts by the authors and quoted interviewees, not the companies or organizations that they represent.

Contributor Bios

Diana Barrett
Data Officer (State Government)

Diana builds data governance and privacy structures from scratch. She managed data in the private, non-profit, and government sectors and currently leads data strategy, governance, and privacy as a Data Officer at a state government agency. Directing the inception of governance and privacy models, she is charged with leadership over agency-wide data activities related to strategy, ownership, accessibility, security, quality, sharing, and use of data. Diana has a legal background and is a Certified Data Management Professional.

Valerie Bonventre Calvo

Vice President of Data Governance & Enablement (Financial Services)

Valerie Calvo is the Vice President of Data Governance & Enablement at BankUnited, where she is developing and helping to realize the data transformation strategy and data & AI governance frameworks. Prior to joining BankUnited, Valerie led global data governance teams at CBRE Investment Management and Bloomberg LP.

She is CDMP accredited with a Master's designation in Data Management and holds Certificates in the Data Management Capability Assessment Model (DCAM) v2.2 (EDM Council) and Advanced Data Analytics (General Assembly). Valerie is also an attorney admitted to practice in New York and New Jersey.

Tiankai Feng

Data & AI Strategy Director (Consulting/Professional Services)

Tiankai is a data leader by day, a musician by night, and an optimist at heart. He is the author of "Humanizing Data Strategy", and is currently working as the Director for Data & AI Strategy at Thoughtworks. With over 12 years of experience in Data Analytics, Data Governance and Data Strategy, he found a passion for the human aspect of data: how to collaborate, communicate and be creative around data. He is passionate about making data more understood, approachable and fun through unconventional methods like music and memes.

John (Hyun Ki) Lee

Associate Director of Data Governance (Financial Services)

With more than a decade of experience in the data realm, John is a seasoned data governance professional dedicated to advocating for the importance of data governance. Passionate about enabling the value of data, he employs a unique approach to enlighten and engage others in the data governance journey. He continues to shape the data landscape, ensuring data integrity and compliance while maximizing its potential for innovation and growth. John has experience from the fast-paced sell-side of the investment industry, working with stakeholders that are looking for velocity without compromising for integrity. He has also held multiple roles on the buy-side of the business, working with much more complex data relationships and developing a deep understanding of the intricacies of the investment world and the value that data can unlock.

Danette McGilvray
Data Governance Expert and Author (Cross Industry)

Danette McGilvray is president and principal of Granite Falls Consulting, a firm that helps organizations increase their success by addressing the information quality and data governance aspects of their business efforts. Focusing on bottom-line results, Granite Falls' strength is in helping clients connect their business strategy to practical steps for implementation. Granite Falls also emphasizes the inclusion of communication, change management, and other human aspects in data quality and governance work.

Danette is the author of *Executing Data Quality Projects: Ten Steps to Quality Data and Trusted Information™, 2nd Ed.* (Elsevier/Academic Press, 2021). An internationally respected expert, Danette's Ten Steps™ approach to data quality has been embraced as a proven method for creating, managing, and sustaining data quality in any organization. The book is used in university graduate programs and has been translated into Chinese and Japanese, with the Spanish translation currently underway. Danette is a co-author of "The Leader's Data Manifesto", a document used to raise awareness about treating data as a business asset. She has overseen its translation into 24 languages. For more information about Danette and Granite Falls see www.gfalls.com. Connect with her on LinkedIn: linkedin.com/in/danette-mcgilvray.

Maria Alejandra Restrepo
Data Governance Manager (Technology)

Alejandra is dedicated to sharing knowledge about data governance and AI governance, fostering a data-driven culture, and empowering the data community in Colombia. She is a Certified Data Management Professional with extensive experience in designing and implementing enterprise-level data governance and management strategies across organizations.

Alejandra has successfully led the development of end-to-end governance frameworks, ensuring data accessibility, quality, and security while fostering a culture that treats data as a critical business asset. She is also a passionate advocate for data literacy, designing initiatives to empower teams with the knowledge and skills to leverage data effectively. Additionally, she has pioneered the implementation of data governance programs through gamification-based approaches, enhancing engagement and driving adoption across organizations.

With strong leadership, strategic thinking, and problem-solving skills, Alejandra effectively guides teams, prioritizes projects based on organizational objectives, and drives the adoption of best practices in data governance.

David Smith

Data Governance Director (Footwear/Apparel)

David Smith is a passionate advocate for data governance and has dedicated his career to helping organizations harness the power of their data while mitigating risks and ensuring compliance. Before data governance was a "thing", he was providing data governance support and leadership in organizations and didn't know how cool the area of data governance would be. With a background in operations and technology,

David brings a unique perspective to his role as the Director of Data Governance at New Balance Athletics, Inc., where he leads efforts to establish and maintain comprehensive data governance for the organization with the support of a great team. He has extensive experience helping complex organizations navigate, achieve, and maintain compliance with data policies and processes. He likes to remind team members in all organizations that data is easy and that we should concentrate on ensuring there are good processes in place.

David holds a Bachelor's in Management of Information Technology, an MBA, and a Master's in Operations and Project Management. When not making a better data world, David can be found with his wife, Sara, and their four daughters, Ana, Mo, Ardyn, and Lo-Lo, enjoying living life in a small town.

Gwen Thomas

Founder, The Data Governance Institute

Gwen Thomas is best known as the Founder of the Data Governance Institute, the primary author of the DGI framework and guidance published at DataGovernance.com, and as a teacher who has influenced hundreds of data programs around the globe. She spent many years working in IT shops and providing data management and data governance consulting services, before spending 10 years as an in-house data strategist for the World Bank Group's private sector arm. Much of her time there focused on translating between executives, program leaders, data governance teams, lawyers, architects, modelers, policy writers, auditors, and data quality teams. Her special focus is on helping non-technical teams become stronger advocates for their own needs.

Appendix

RAPID Model for Decision-Making

The RAPID Model helps clarify decision accountability. Recommend, Agree, Perform, Input, and Decide assign owners to the five key roles in any decision.

*Note that while the acronym RAPID is easy to remember, the roles do NOT happen in the order they appear.

People who 'Recommend' are responsible for:

- Providing a proposal on the decision
- Providing data and analysis to make a sensible choice in a timely fashion
- Consulting with 'input' people, making sure their views are considered, and ensuring their commitment.

People who 'Agree' are responsible for:

- Negotiating a modified plan with the 'Recommender' if necessary
- Escalating any decisions that can't be resolved between the Agreer and the Recommender to the 'Decider'
- Exercising their veto power over the recommendation, if necessary.

People who 'Perform' are responsible for:

- Acting on the decision once it's made
- Ensuring the decision is implemented effectively and appropriately.

People who 'Input' are responsible for:

- Sheding light on the project's practical implications, including risks, to the Recommender.

People who 'Decide' are responsible for:

- Serving as the single point of accountability
- Making a final decision and resolving any conflict in the decision-making process
- Ensuring that the resources required to implement this project are provided.

Models for Change Management

Here is a list of some commonly used change management models. You can find many articles on the internet explaining these models. We discussed the preference for the ANCHOR change leadership model as compared to these models in Section B. The ANCHOR model is relevant for middle managers who lead data governance change initiatives, as explained throughout this book.

Kotter 8-Step Change Model

Lewin's Change Management Model

McKinsey 7-S model

Kotter's theory: Coaching people through change

The 'Nudge' Theory of Change Management

The 5-goals ADKAR for Successful Change Management

Bridges' Transition Model

Kübler-Ross Change Curve

The Satir Change Management Model

The table below compares the top 6 models to the ANCHOR model, showing the clear need for the ANCHOR model.

2. Table: A Summary of Change Management Models

S No	Model Title	Reference	Key Features	Features Missing	Middle-manager Focus
1	McKinsey 7 S	Channon & Caldart (2015)	Shared Values as the core and Strategy, Structure, Systems, Style, Staff, and Skills as the six features running off the core feature	1. Employee behavior change is assumed through the updating of shared values 2. The change may be implemented only after successful	No mention of a middle management role. The model seems to be driven by top management, who alone may change the shared values

S No	Model Title	Reference	Key Features	Features Missing	Middle-manager Focus
				shared value updates	for the entire organization.
2	ADKAR	Hiatt (2006)	Assumes the individual behavior model is separate from the change operationalization model.	1. May need a centralized project team to coordinate the two models 2. Change management follows a successful behavior modification. That may require multiple iterations.	No mention of a middle management role. The senior managers must play a key role as coordination is required at a central point.
3	3-perspective	Anderson and Anderson (2010)	3-perspectives: content, people, and processes 9-phase Change Leader's Roadmap: 1. Preparing to Lead the Change Initiative, 2. Defining the Organizational Vision, Commitment and strengthening the Capabilities, 3. Determine the Design Requirements by Assessing the Situation, 4. Enabling the achievement of the Vision by Creating the Desired Design State, 5.Analysis of the Impact, 6.Masterminding the	It is a complex model that offers many alternatives from which to choose. May be relevant for experts in change management. Does not provide an easy-to-follow path for middle managers.	No mention of a middle management role.

S No	Model Title	Reference	Key Features	Features Missing	Middle-manager Focus
			implementation plans, integrating various actions for achieving efficiencies and optimizing resource utilization, 7.Implementing the Change Plans, 8. Celebrating as well as Integrating the New State, 9. Learning and Correct Course		
4	Kotter's Change Manageme nt Model	Applebaum et al. (2012)	1. Establish a sense of urgency for the change initiative, 2. create a guiding coalition, 3. develop a vision and strategy, 4. communicate the change vision, 5. empower broad-based action, 6. generate short-term wins, 7. consolidate gains and produce more change, and 8. anchor new approaches in the corporate culture	1. A rigid approach - sequential. 2. Some steps are not required in certain contexts. 3. Does not address resistance and commitment to change. 4. Maybe suitable for large, organization-wide change but not small changes focused on a couple of departments.	No mention of a middle management role
5	Bridge's Transition Model	Bridges (2009)	Phase1. Letting go of the old ways and old identity people	1. It is a broad framework and does not suggest	No mention of a middle

S No	Model Title	Reference	Key Features	Features Missing	Middle-manager Focus
			had. Help people with losses. Phase2. The in-between time when the old is gone and the new is not fully operational. Time for psychological realignments. Phase3. Coming out of transition and making a new beginning. People develop new identities and a sense of new purpose.	specific steps to manage change. 2. The model's focus is on behavior change. Does not cover any other area of change management.	management role
6	Kubler Ross Change Curve	Chavan & Bhattacharya (2022)	Five stages of psychological behavior: Denial, Anger, Bargaining, Depression, Acceptance	Focuses on resistance to change, and not the whole change process.	No mention of a middle management role.

References

Anderson, L. A., & Anderson, D. (2010). *The change leader's roadmap: How to navigate your organization's transformation.* John Wiley & Sons, Hoboken, N.J.

Appelbaum, S. H., Habashy, S., Malo, J. L., & Shafiq, H. (2012). Back to the future: revisiting Kotter's 1996 change model. *Journal of Management Development, 31*(8), 764-782.

Bridges, W. (2009). *Managing transitions: Making the most of change.* Da Capo Press.

Channon, D. F., & Caldart, A. A. (2015). McKinsey 7S model. *Wiley encyclopedia of management,* 1-1.

Chavan, S., & Bhattacharya, S. (2022). Study of employees' behavior during organizational change: effects of business theatre on Kübler-Ross model. *Cardiometry*(22), 237-243.

Hiatt, J. M. (2006). *ADKAR: A model for change in business, government and our community: How to implement successful change in our personal lives and professional careers.* Prosci Research.

Further Resources

Handouts, list of resources, and other material in relation to this book can be found on AnchorYourChange.com

Index